TALMUD OF JMMANUEL

by Judas Iscariot

The Clear Translation in English

Translation of the Aramaic scrolls written by Judas Iscariot, the disciple of Jmmanuel (Jesus), discovered in 1963 by Eduard Albert Meier in the tomb where Jmmanuel had lain for three days.

ISBN 13 digit: 978-1-893157-12-5
ISBN 10 digit: 1-893157-12-1

Published by

BRIDGER HOUSE PUBLISHERS, INC

P.O. Box 2208, Carson City, NV 89702, USA

1-800-729-4131

Layout by therighttype.com

Printed in the United States of America

10 9 8 7 6 5 4 3 2 1

Table of Contents

Foreword

In 1963 the text presented in this book was discovered by "Billy" Eduard Albert Meier in the form of scrolls encased in preservative resin, after a Greek Catholic priest by the name of Isa Rashid discovered the actual burial cave of Jmmanuel (who has been erroneously called Jesus Christ). Written in the literary language of Old Aramaic, the document was buried under a flat rock in the tomb. It was Rashid's wish that his name not be publicized. He feared, and rightfully so, that he would be persecuted by the Church and the Israelis and perhaps even be assassinated, a possibility that unfortunately became true later.

The author of the scrolls was a contemporary and disciple of Jmmanuel who was known by the name of Judas Iscariot. For about 2000 years he has been wrongly denounced as the traitor of Jmmanuel, although he had nothing to do with the betrayal. This ugly deed was actually carried out by Juda Ihariot, the son of a Pharisee.

In order to save their threatened heresy, today's still-dominant orthodox and conservative clergy and their naive followers will probably attempt to deny the scrolls, destroy this book and denounce it as lies, as they have done with many other ancient writings that bore witness to the truth. (See, for example, the books Henoch and Jezihra, among others, which were removed from the Bible because they had been too close to the truth when handed down. As before, it will happen again that this writing will be attacked and probably taken out of circulation. It will probably happen that pressure from many sides will be exercised on the editor of the writing, or he may be persecuted or assassinated in order to preserve the "true religion." (Three attempts on his life were made in 1976, once even in the presence of witnesses. By the end of 1990 the number of murder attempts had increased to 13.) Certainly efforts will be made to induce police, authorities, public prosecutors, judges and courts of all kinds to prohibit this book, to ridicule it, to repudiate it or to suppress it, actions which, however, will not detract one iota from its veracity. The obscurantists in charge certainly will proceed with all circumspection, skill and intrigues to have the document dismissed, denounced as a hoax and quashed, as has been the case upon publication of other writings whose original scripts, however, were then hidden in the Vatican Library in Rome.

But there will also ensue an outcry against the text from the religious fanatics and other misled persons who will want to proceed with all means against its existence and the editor. It has always been like that, as everyone knows — there is no shying away from murder, assassination or anything similar. The editor is well acquainted with this fact and consequently has taken necessary precautions. But the "Holy Ministry," the "Holy See in Rome" and the Pope have always taken steps to build up or to save the erroneous cult religion of Christianity. In this connection the readers need only to think of the Inquisition (ordered by the "Holy See"), through whose command millions of people in Europe done were brutally slaughtered, tortured and murdered. The number of murders on record committed by the "Holy See" amounted to nine million during the Inquisition, while the number of undocumented murders adds at least another nine million.

This translation provides strong evidence that the cult religions' heretic doctrines have manipulated the truth and that they are the irresponsible machinations of unscrupulous men, some of whom were hired by the "Holy See." Others were foolish, fanatical, in a deranged state of consciousness, or power-hungry human beings who, without hesitation or scruple, misled humanity for thousands of years, shedding the blood of millions through murder. Furthermore, the descendants of these murderers and unscrupulous men established over the centuries and millennia a mighty cult-religious power capable of ruling over all humanity. In the course of past millennia the cult religions ruthlessly, and through bloody and brutal murders, fought their way to become the most powerful forces of the earth, to which even brutal and dictatorial governments bowed down and still do.

Cult Religion:

The most sordid pretext of maximum power in the name of false and mendacious love that literally walks over dead bodies without hesitation or scruple.

Backed by the false doctrine of the New Testament, the Christian cult religion meddles in the politics of all countries. Moreover, it is not embarrassed to interfere in the most intimate family life of human beings — even in the bed of marriage partners — in order even there to attack and destroy the last and most private secrets of human beings.

Now finally has come the time when a stop can be put to all these unscrupulous activities, if man becomes sensible enough, revises his thinking and devotes himself to the real teachings of Jmmanuel. In all likelihood, all those who have bashed their heads against the brick wall of the cult religions' deceitful madness and are therefore no longer capable of normal and sensible thinking, will fight and oppose it with all means; and yet, their desperate fight will be in vain because truth will be stronger than any cult-religious mania or dirty lie, even though the lie has been in existence for thousands of years. The scandalous falsehoods of cult religions will now be shattered and destroyed for good, no matter how much the cult religions and all their followers and advocates rebel against it. Finally truth will be victorious, even though it must be secured through great struggles, as it has been written in the Scriptures, which say that the truth will provoke a worldwide catastrophe. However, truth is required and must no longer be silenced. A catastrophe will be understandable if one considers that the cult religions have attained immense power, which so far has enabled them to suppress, with murderous and sordid means, all truths directed against them. They will again attempt to do this, even if it means indulging in murder as has often been the case in the past. For this reason, the editor of this work will run the risk of being persecuted by order of the cult religions, private fanatics and sect members to be murdered or be handed over to the courts.

From all this may the earthling at last realize what the cult religions are and with what type of bloody means they fight the truth, as it is only in this way that they are capable of maintaining their full power and control over the enslaved human beings.

Here it must be pointed out emphatically that followers and supporters of the true teachings of Jmmanuel are just as much at risk as is the editor of this document himself. However, the editor is even more endangered because he is the contact man for extraterrestrial intelligences and very highly developed spiritual entities on exalted planes who transmit to him true spiritual teachings that he disseminates without modification, thereby exposing the lies of the cult religions, which will lead to their slow but certain eradication.

Isa Rashid, the discoverer of the burial cave and translator of the original scrolls, was equally endangered, so that years earlier he took the precaution of withdrawing from the Church to live incognito somewhere with the family he had started in the interim. Conscious of the immense power of the cult religions, he wanted to conceal both his name and the original scripts from the public. He rightfully feared for his life and for those of his beloved family, all of whom since that time have become victims of the cult religions' persecutors, by whom they were assassinated. Long before this point in time, Rashid, under the seal of secrecy that his name not be mentioned, gave the translation of the scrolls to his good friend, the editor, Eduard Meier. But it was not until 1974 that Meier, in turn, received permission from the plane of Arahat Athersata to make the translation of the scrolls accessible to other interested circles.

In 1963, Rashid on various occasions took his friend, Eduard Meier, to the actual burial cave of Jmmanuel, which was practically filled with a great deal of sand and dirt. In the course of excavations Meier subsequently found various items that confirmed the contents of the scripts.

Unfortunately it must be mentioned that the document is no longer complete, since various pieces of the scrolls were completely illegible and decayed. Furthermore, some were obviously missing. What was preserved nevertheless bears showing witness that in the course of two millennia an infamous false doctrine, a web of unequaled lies, was manufactured around the person of Jmmanuel in order to erect a cult-religious power and unscrupulously enslave earthlings — all this truly at the cost of misled, trusting and unaware human beings and their belongings, and above all at the cost of innocently spilled blood through the dirty intrigues of the "Holy See," which deceitfully preaches love for the purpose of exploitation, enslavement and assault of people on Earth.

It is very rare that one individual succeeds in publicizing themes and truths that clarify causal connections or at the least shed some light on them when they pertain to cult religions or political matters. The existing practice proves that, as a rule, such human beings were unscrupulously persecuted, tortured and murdered. Forces called to the fore appear promptly, knowing how to place the truthful contents of a statement into a dim light. To them any means is justifiable to make truth itself into a travesty. But that is not all, because as soon as anything is published and disseminated that clarifies causal relationships and truths concerning cult religions or political matters, then, the publications are taken out of circulation with the help of clergy, police, government agencies, courts, the powerful of the cult religions and their fanatical followers. The publications are "safeguarded" or destroyed, to continue depriving the earthling of the real truth, letting him starve and perish woefully in his misery of false thinking and false teachings, because only in so doing can he be further exploited to his last drop of blood, particularly by governments and cult religions.

The editor,
"Billy" Eduard Albert Meier

Chapter 1

The Genealogical Tree of Jmmanuel

1:1 This is the book and mystery of Jmmanuel, which means "the one with godly knowledge," who is a son of Joseph, of Jacob, the distant descendant of David, who was a descendant of Abraham, whose lineage traces back to Adam, the father of one of Earth's human races, who was begotten by Semjasa, the leader of the celestial sons who were the guardian angels of god, the great ruler of the distant travelers.

1:2 Semjasa, the celestial son and guardian angel of god, the great ruler of the distant travelers who traversed the expanse of the universe, together with a terrestrial woman, begot Adam, the father of the white human race.

1:3 Adam took for himself an earth wife and begot Seth.

1:4 Seth begot Enos.

1:5 Enos begot Akjbeel.

1:6 Akjbeel begot Aruseak.

1:7 Aruseak begot Kenan.

1:8 Kenan begot Mahalaleel.

1:9 Mahalaleel begot Urakjbarameel.

1:10 Urakjbarameel begot Jared.

1:11 Jared begot Enoch.

1:12 Enoch begot Methusalah.

1:13 Methusalah begot Lamech.

1:14 Lamech begot Tamjel.

1:15 Tamjel begot Danel.

1:16 Danel begot Asael.

1:17 Asael begot Samsafeel.

1:18 Samsafeel begot Jomjael.

1:19 Jomjael begot Turel.

1:20 Turel begot Hamech.

1:21 Hamech begot Noah.

1:22 Noah begot Sem.

1:23 Sem begot Arpachsad.

1:24 Arpachsad begot Batraal.

1:25 Batraal begot Ramuel.

1:26 Ramuel begot Askeel.

1:27 Askeel begot Armers.

1:28 Armers begot Salah.

1:29 Salah begot Eber.

1:30 Eber begot Peleg.

1:31 Peleg begot Regu.

1:32 Regu begot Serug.

1:33 Serug begot Araseal.

1:34 Araseal begot Nahor.

1:35 Nahor begot Thara.

1:36 Thara begot Abraham.

1:37 Abraham begot Jsaak.

1:38 Jsaak begot Jacob.

1:39 Jacob begot Juda.

1:40 Juda begot Ananj.

1:41 Ananj begot Ertael.

1:42 Ertael begot Perez.

1:43 Perez begot Hezron.

1:44 begot Ram.

1:45 Ram begot Amjnadab.

1:46 Amjnadab begot Savebe.

1:47 Savebe begot Nahesson.

1:48 Nahesson begot Sahna.

1:49 Sahna begot Boas.

1:50 Boas begot Obed.

1:51 Obed begot Jesse.

1:52 Jesse begot Davjd.

1:53 Davjd begot Solomon.

1:54 Solomon begot Asa.

1:55 begot Gadaeel.

1:56 Gadaeel begot Josaphat.

1:57 Josaphat begot Jora.

1:58 Jora begot Armeneel.

1:59 Armeneel begot Usja.

1:60 Usja begot Jothan.

1:61 Jothan begot Gadreel.

1:62 Gadreel begot Ahas.

1:63 Ahas begot Jtjskja.

1:64 Jtjskja begot Manasse.

1:65 Manasse begot Amon.

1:66 Amon begot Josja.

1:67 Josja begot Jojachjn.

1:68 Jojachjn begot Sealthjel.

1:69 Sealthjel begot Jequn.

1:70 Jequn begot Serubabel.

1:71 Serubabel begot Abjud.

1:72 Abjud begot Eljakjm.

1:73 Eljakjm begot Asor.

1:74 Asor begot Zadok.

1:75 Zadok begot Achjm.

1:76 Achjm begot Eljud.

1:77 Eljud begot Eleasar.

1:78 Eleasar begot Matthan.

1:79 Matthan begot Jacob.

1:80 Jacob begot Joseph.

1:81 Joseph was the husband of Mary, the mother of Jmmanuel, who became pregnant by a distant descendant of the celestial son, Rasiel, who was the guardian angel of the secret.

1:82 When Joseph heard of Mary's secret impregnation by a descendant of the celestial sons, from the lineage of Rasiel, behold, he was filled with wrath and thought of leaving Mary, before he would be married to her in front of the people.

1:83 While Joseph was thinking in this manner, behold, a guardian angel, sent by the celestial son, Gabriel, who had impregnated Mary, appeared and said,

1:84 "Joseph, Mary is betrothed to you and you are her consort; do not leave her, because the fruit of her womb is chosen for a great purpose. Marry her in all candor, so that you may be husband and wife before the people.

1:85 "Behold, the impregnation of Mary occurred eleven thousand years after the procreation of Adam through the celestial son, Semjasa, to fulfill the word of god, the ruler of those who traveled from afar, who said through the prophet Isaiah,

1:86 "'Behold, a virgin will be impregnated by a celestial son before she is married to a man before the people.

1:87 "'They will name the fruit of her womb Jmmanuel, which translated means 'the one with godly knowledge,' as a symbol and honor to god, through whose power and providential care the earth was made to bear intelligent human life, through the pairing of the women of earth with the celestial sons, the distant travelers of the universe.'

1:88 "Behold, god and his followers came from out of the depths of space, delivering themselves from a strong bondage, and creating a new race and home with the early women of this earth.

1:89 "God deserves the honor of people of earth, for behold: He is the true originator of the white and of the colored human races of Earth, and to him honor should be given.

1:90 "There is no form comparable to him for this human race created by him; therefore, people should have no other gods besides him, who created other human races in other parts of the earth.

1:91 "Outside of god there is nothing of comparable form worthy of reputation. Only the omnipotence of all creation reigns over him and his celestial sons: Creation itself, which should be revered.

1:92 "Behold, therefore; over the earth reigns god, the master of the celestial sons and the people of the white and of the colored races.

1:93 "God is the lawgiver of this human race, and therefore, his wishes should be fulfilled by man and woman.

1:94 "God, the lord, is generous in his love, but also terrible in his anger when his laws are disobeyed.

1:95 "Mary's impregnation is god's law, so you, Joseph, are to be her husband in matrimony."

The Birth of Jmmanuel

1:96 Joseph, however, when he heard that, was mindful of his devoutness to god's laws, so he brought Mary home and married her before the people.

1:97 At that time a decree went out from Emperor Augustus, that all the world should be taxed.

1:98 This census was the first of its kind and occurred at the time that Cyrenius was governor in Syria.

1:99 All went to their own towns, so that they could be counted.

1:100 Joseph of Galilee, of the town of Nazareth, also went with his wife Mary to the Judaic land of the city of David, which is called Bethlehem, because he was of the house and lineage of David,

1:101 in order to be counted with his wife Mary, who was pregnant by the celestial son Gabriel from the lineage of Rasiel.

1:102 When they were there, the time came for her to give birth.

1:103 Since they could find no shelter, they spent the night in a stable.

1:104 And Mary bore her first son in the straw, wrapped him in cloth, and put him in a manger near the animals, because otherwise there was no room in the inn.

Chapter 2

The Wise Men from the Orient

2:1 When Jmmanuel was born in the stable at Bethlehem, in the shelter in the land of the Judeans at the time of Herod Antipas, Tetrarch of Galilee and Peraea, behold, there came wise men from the Orient to Jerusalem, saying,

2:2a "Where is the newborn king of wisdom of the Judeans?

2:2b "We have seen a bright light in the sky and heard a voice saying,

2:3 "'Follow the tail of the light, because the king of wisdom of the Judeans is born, who will bring great knowledge.'

2:4 "Therefore we have come to adore the newborn king of wisdom.

2:5 "He shall possess the knowledge of god and be a son of the celestial son Gabriel.

2:6 "His knowledge will be boundless and his power will rule the spirit of human beings, so that they may learn and serve Creation."

2:7 When Herod Antipas heard this, he was frightened, and with him all of Jerusalem, because they feared that the newborn child might exercise dreadful power.

2:8 Herod Antipas called together all the chief priests and scribes among the people and inquired of them where Jmmanuel had been born.

2:9 And they said to him, "In Bethlehem, in the Judean land; for thus it is written by the prophet Micah:

2:10 "'And you, Bethlehem, in the land of the Judeans, are by no means the least among the cities in Judea, for out of you shall come the king of wisdom, who will bring great knowledge to the people of Israel so that they may learn and serve Creation.'"

2:11 Thereupon, Herod Antipas called the wise men secretly and diligently inquired of them when the bright light with the long tail had appeared in the sky.

2:12 Later he directed them to Bethlehem, saying, "Go and search diligently for the young child, and when you find him, let me know so that I may come and adore him."

2:13 When they had heard Herod Antipas, they departed. And behold, the light with the long tail, which they had seen in the Orient, went ahead of them with a high-pitched singing sound until it came to Bethlehem and stood directly over the stable where the infant was born.

2:14 When they saw this they rejoiced.

2:15 They went into the stable and found the young child with his mother, Mary, and Joseph. They fell down and worshiped the infant and offered their treasures, which were gold, frankincense and myrrh.

2:16 However, the voice again rang out from the light high above, saying that they should not return to Herod Antipas because he planned evil for the young child.

2:17 So they returned to their country by another route.

2:18 After the three wise men had left, behold, the celestial son Gabriel appeared to Joseph, saying,

2:19 "Rise and take the infant and his mother Mary with you and flee to Egypt. Stay there until I tell you, because Herod Antipas is planning to seek out the young child to kill him, since he fears that the little child might wield terrible power.

2:20 "While you are in Egypt, I will send my messenger to Herod Antipas to teach him the truth."

2:21 And Joseph rose and took the young child and his mother by night and escaped under the guidance of the celestial son Gabriel in the descending light, which fled to Egypt along with them.

2:22 They remained there until Herod Antipas had a change of mind and the fear in him abated.

2:23 When Herod Antipas saw that he had nothing to fear from the young boy to whom only great wisdom and knowledge was attributed, he felt safe within his realm. Thus, he promised the ambassador of the celestial son Gabriel not to pursue Mary, Joseph and Jmmanuel further.

2:24 When Herod Antipas and his followers had had a change of mind, behold, the celestial son Gabriel appeared again before Joseph in Egypt, saying,

2:25 "Arise and take the young child and his mother Mary and move back to the land of Israel; all those who sought the child's life have had a change of heart."

2:26 And Joseph rose, took the child and his mother, and returned into the light that had once more appeared; it took them to Israel.

2:27 The celestial son Gabriel took them back into the land of Galilee.

2:28 There they dwelled in the city called Nazareth, so that what was spoken by the prophets might be fulfilled: "Jmmanuel shall be called the Nazarene."

Chapter 3

John the Baptist

3:1 John the Baptist came at a certain time to the edge of the wilderness, preaching at the banks of the Jordan.

3:2 He preached the baptism according to the old laws of god, according to which the way to knowledge was to be prepared.

3:3 He preached that god's laws have to be followed because he is the only ruler for this human race.

3:4 He preached that above god, however, stands Creation, the maker of the worlds, universes and all living things.

3:5 And so he taught that the genderless Creation is the secret of all secrets: death and life, light and darkness, being and non-being.

3:6 And so he taught once again that god, the lord, the ruler of this human race and of those who traveled from afar, the celestial sons, holds Creation in high esteem.

3:7 All Judea and all the people of Jerusalem went out to John the Baptist, acknowledging the wisdom of the old laws of god and allowing him to baptize them in the river Jordan.

3:8 John had a coat of camel's hair and a leather belt around his loins; his food was locusts and wild honey.

3:9 When he was baptizing many of the people, there came many Pharisees and Sadducees to him, taunting him with malicious talk.

3:10 But John the Baptist spoke, "You brood of vipers, who told you that you will escape from future wrath, once your false teachings are detected?

3:11 "See to it that you bear righteous fruit of repentance and learn the truth.

3:12 "Turn away from the evil of your false teachings, which you carry out with arrogance and motivations of your power and greed.

3:13 "Do not think just of saying to each other: 'We have Abraham as father.'

3:14 "I say to you, god is able, with his knowledge and his power, to raise up children to Abraham out of these stones, because he knows about the secret of Creation.

3:15 "Already the axe has been laid to the root of the trees. Therefore, any tree that does not bring forth good fruit will be hewn down and thrown into the fire.

3:16 "You brood of vipers, in two times a thousand years you and your descendants, who carry on false teaching out of your own pride from motives of power and greed, shall be punished and your lies destroyed.

3:17 "So it will be when the human race begins to comprehend and separate the wheat from the chaff.

3:18 "The time will be when your false teachings will be laughed at and the human race finds the truth.

3:19 "So it will happen when the human race builds singing lights and fire wagons, with which they can move into outer space, as is done by god and his followers, the celestial sons,

3:20 "namely those who taught us the wisdom and knowledge of Creation,

3:21 "and who urge us to obey the law of nature and live according to it.

3:22 "Oh you renegades, you brood of vipers, get away from this place, because you are impure and cursed in your false teachings.

3:23 "Get away from this place, because I can by my own accord baptize you into repentance only with water; but he who comes after me is stronger than I, and I am not worthy to take off his sandals. He will baptize you with the knowledge of the spirit and with the fire of truth.

3:24 "He has his winnowing fork in his hand; he will sweep his threshing floor and gather the wheat into his granary, but he will burn the chaff with unquenchable fire.

3:25 "The lie can never withstand the truth, which destroys evil in its fire."

3:26 As John the Baptist thus spoke, behold, Jmmanuel of Galilee then came to him at the Jordan, to be baptized by him.

3:27 John, however, refused him and spoke, "I certainly need to be baptized by you, because you possess greater knowledge than I, and you come to me?"

3:28 But Jmmanuel answered him, "Let it happen so now, because it is fitting for us to fulfill all justice, since we are both sons of the earth."

3:29 So John consented and baptized him.

3:30 When Jmmanuel had been baptized, he soon came out of the water of the Jordan, and behold, a metallic light dropped from the sky and descended steeply over the Jordan.

3:31 Consequently they all fell on their faces and pressed them into the sand while a voice from the metallic light spoke,

3:32 "This is my beloved son with whom I am well pleased. He will be the king of truth who will lift this human race to knowledge."

3:33 Behold, after these words Jmmanuel entered into the metallic light, which climbed into the sky, surrounded by fire and smoke, and passed over the lifeless sea, as the singing of the metallic light soon faded away.

3:34 After that, Jmmanuel was no longer seen for forty days and nights.

Chapter 4

The Secret of Jmmanuel

4:1 From this day on Jmmanuel no longer lived among humankind of these human races.

4:2 Jmmanuel was lifted up from the earth, and no one knew where he had been taken or what had happened to him.

4:3 But then he was let off by the metallic light between North and West, where the guardian angels had received cords with which they had to measure the place for the chosen ones.

4:4 Thus, he lived for forty days and nights between the winds of the north and the west, where he received the secret of knowledge.

4:5 Meanwhile, he spent his days with the wise saints of god and with the guardian angels, the celestial sons.

4:6 They taught him the wisdom of knowledge.

4:7 They taught him the dominion of god over this human race and his celestial sons.

4:8 They also explained to him the omnipotence of the Creation of the universes.

4:9 They also taught him about the immortality of the spirit through rebirth.

4:10 There he saw the forefathers, the saints of ancient times, who were the fathers of the human races, the celestial sons.

4:11 From there he went to the North at the ends of the earth, where the metallic lights and fire wagons rushed out of the sky or, singing, shot up into the sky, covered with smoke and fire.

4:12 There, at the ends of the entire earth, he saw a great and marvelous wonder.

4:13 Here, he saw the celestial gates open, of which there were three different ones.

4:14 The celestial gates radiated in brightest Sohar an area great as the lifeless sea near the river Jordan.

4:15 Actually radiating therein was the whole land of Israel, alive and true, humans and animals and everything that was there.

4:16 In this first celestial gate, there was no concealed secret, because the Sohar entered into the smallest room of the cottages and revealed the last hidden thing.

4:17 Inside the second celestial gate, there rose mighty mountains, whose tops reached into the sky and disappeared into the clouds.

4:18 Far below lay deep masses of snow, at whose edges another human race, of brown skin, built their huts.

4:19 The third celestial portal revealed a land of gigantic dimensions, mountainous and interspersed with rivers, lakes and seas, where again another human race dwelled.

4:20 Not far from these three celestial gates was the palace of god, the ruler of these human races and those who had traveled from afar, the celestial sons, or guardian angels.

4:21 In his palace god ruled over the three human races created by him and over his following, the celestial sons.

4:22 He was immortal, ancient and of giant size like the celestial sons.

4:23 In the palace of god there appeared to Jmmanuel two very tall men, the likes of which he had never seen on earth.

4:24 Their faces shone like the sun, and their eyes looked like burning torches. Out of their mouths issued fire. Their clothing resembled a covering of foam, and their arms were like golden wings.

4:25 They lived in their own world, because the air of this earthly world would have killed them.

4:26 These two men from the constellation of the seven stars The Pleiades were venerable teachers and were together with two smaller men who said that they were from Baawi.

4:27 They said, "People have come from the heavens to earth, and other people have been lifted from earth into the heavens, and the people coming from the heavens remained on earth a long time and have created the intelligent human races.

4:28 "Behold, humans begotten by the celestial sons were different in a specific way from other people on Earth.

4:29 "They were not like Earth humans, but like the children of the celestial angels, a different kind.

4:30 "Their bodies were white as snow and red as the rose blossom, their hair at the top of the head white as wool and their eyes beautiful.

4:31 "The human races will now retain their inherited beauty and propagate it further.

4:32 "But in the course of centuries and millennia they will mix with other races of the earth and the heavens, so as to generate new human races and special lineages, as the celestial sons did with the Earth people.

4:33 "Jmmanuel, you are in on the secret, begotten from among our ranks by a celestial son.

4:34 "With your knowledge you will make the impossible possible and accomplish things that the human races will attest to as miracles.

4:35 "You know the power of the spirit, but beware of abusing it.

4:36 "Your own wisdom and knowledge obtained through us will contribute to the well-being of the human races, though the road leading thereto will be very difficult for them and you.

4:37 "You will be misunderstood and renounced, because the human races are still ignorant and given to superstition.

4:38 "They believe that god is Creation itself and not the ruler of the celestial sons and these human races.

4:39 "Earth people attribute to him the omnipotence of Creation and glorify him as Creation itself.

4:40 "But god is a person, like all the celestial sons and the human races, except vastly greater in consciousness than they.

4:41 "Creation, however, is of immeasurably higher standing than god, the lord over the celestial sons and human races, because Creation is the immeasurable secret.

4:42 "Jmmanuel, they will also taunt you as god and his only-begotten son, and you, too, will be set equal to the mysterious Creation.

4:43 "Nevertheless, do not heed these false teachings, because millennia will pass before the people of these human races will be able to recognize the truth.

4:44 "Much human blood will be shed on your account, yours as well as that of countless generations.

4:45 "Notwithstanding, fulfill your mission as the king of wisdom, as the son of Gabriel, the celestial son.

4:46 "In the name of god the law was issued to create you so that you may serve as prophet and pioneer of wisdom for these human races.

4:47 "Fulfill your mission unperturbed in the face of irrationality, disbelieving people and false teachings of the scribes and Pharisees.

4:48 "Hence, following the fulfillment of your mission, centuries and two millennia will pass before the truth of your knowledge brought among the people will be recognized and disseminated by some humans.

4:49 "Not until the time of space-traveling machines will the truth break through and gradually shake the false teaching that you are the son of god or Creation.

4:50 "However, this will be the time when we celestial sons begin to reveal ourselves anew to the human races, since they will have become knowing and with their acquired power threaten the structure of the heavens."

4:51 Thus they spoke, the celestial sons between the North and the West, before they took Jmmanuel in the metallic light back to Israel, to the land of Galilee.

4:52 When Jmmanuel heard that John the Baptist had been imprisoned, he left the town of Nazareth, came and lived in Capernaum, which lies on the sea in the land of Sebulon and Naphtali.

4:53 From that time Jmmanuel began to preach, saying, "Repent and turn to the truth and knowledge, because they alone bring you life!"

4:54 When Jmmanuel went by the Sea of Galilee, he saw two brothers, Simon who is called Peter, and Andrew, his brother, casting their nets into the sea because they were fishermen.

4:55 And he said to them, "Follow me; I will teach you knowledge and make you fishers of men."

4:56 Immediately they left their nets and followed him.

4:57a As he went on farther, he saw two other brothers, Jacob, the son of Zebedee, and John, his brother, in the boat with Zebedee, their father, mending their nets.

4:57b And he called them.

4:58 Immediately they left the boat and their father and followed him.

4:59 Jmmanuel went about in the whole land of Galilee, teaching in their synagogues, preaching the knowledge of the spirit and healing all diseases and infirmities among the people.

4:60 The news of him spread over the whole land of Syria, and they brought to him all the sick, demoniacs, sleepwalkers and paralytics, afflicted with various diseases and torments; and he made them well.

4:61 And many people followed him, from Galilee, from the Decapolis, from Jerusalem, from Judea and from beyond the Jordan.

Chapter 5

The Sermon on the Mount

5:1 When Jmmanuel saw the people following him, he went up a hill and sat down; and his disciples came to him.

5:2 And he taught them, saying,

5:3 "Blessed are those who are rich in spirit and recognize the truth, for life is theirs.

5:4 "Blessed are those who mourn, for they shall thus recognize truth and be comforted.

5:5 "Blessed are the spiritually balanced, for they shall possess knowledge.

5:6 "Blessed are those who hunger and thirst for truth and knowledge, for they shall be satisfied.

5:7 "Blessed are those who live according to the laws of nature, for they live according to the plan of Creation.

5:8 "Blessed are those who have a clear conscience, for they need not fear.

5:9 "Blessed are those who know about Creation, for they do not follow false teachings.

5:10 "Blessed are the righteous, for nature is subject to them.

5:11 "Blessed are you if, on my account and because of our teachings, men revile and persecute you and falsely speak all manner of evil against you.

5:12 "Thus those who belittle the truth have persecuted the prophets who were before you, so rejoice and be of good cheer; life and the next life will reward you.

5:13 "You are the salt of the earth, and if the salt loses its flavor, with what should one salt? It is henceforth useless, except to be thrown out and stepped on by the people.

5:14 "You are the light of the world, and consider: the city that lies on top of a mountain cannot be hidden.

5:15 "Nor does one light a candle and place it under a bushel, but on a candlestick; thus it illuminates all those who are in the house.

5:16 "Likewise your light should shine before the people, so that they see your good works and recognize the truth of your knowledge.

5:17 "Do not think that I have come to abolish the law or the prophets; I have come not to abolish, but to fulfill and to reveal knowledge.

5:18 "Truly, I say to you: Until the heavens and the earth vanish, neither an iota nor a dot of the law of Creation and the laws of nature will vanish, until all has been fulfilled.

5:19 "Whoever violates one of the laws or commandments and teaches the people falsely, will be called the hyprocrites; but whoever spreads the teachings truthfully will be called great and will receive the thanks of the spirit.

5:20 "I tell you: If your righteousness does not exceed that of the scribes and Pharisees, you will not receive the thanks of the spirit and of life.

5:21 "You have heard that it was said to the men of old, 'You should not kill; but whoever kills shall be found guilty by the courts.'

5:22 "However, I say to you: Exercise justice according to the natural law of Creation, so that the judgment is found in logic.

5:23 "Guilty are all who do not act in self-defense or according to a prescribed judgment of the law, if they kill or engage in evil speech and actions.

5:24 "Justice according to the natural laws of Creation alone elevates a verdict into logic.

5:25 "Do not accommodate your adversaries, if you are in the right, and the judge will probably have to decide in your favor.

5:26 "Truly, I say to you: You will achieve justice only when you find it yourself and can make your fellow human understand it.

5:27 "You have heard that it was said, you should not commit adultery.

5:28 "But I say to you: Whoever cohabits with someone other than their spouse should be delivered up to the courts, because it is unworthy of humans, contemptible and an offense to the laws of nature.

5:29 "If, however, your right or left eye causes annoyance, tear it out and throw it away, because it is better for you that just one of your members be destroyed than your whole body.

5:30 "If a thought causes you annoyance, eradicate it and ban it from your brain. It is better to destroy a thought that incites annoyance than to bring the whole world of thought into an uproar.

5:31 "It has also been said, whoever divorces his spouse should hand over a certificate of divorce.

5:32 "However, I say to you: Whoever separates from their spouse, except in case of adultery, causes the marriage to break; whoever marries a divorced person that is guilty also commits adultery.

5:33 "You have further heard it said to the men of old, you shall take no false oath and keep your oath to god.

5:34 "However, I say to you that you should not swear at all; swear not by the heavens, because they are infinite and immeasurable.

5:35 "Neither swear by the Earth, because it is impermanent, nor swear by Jerusalem, because it is an impermanent city built by the hand of man.

5:36 "You should also not swear by your head, because you cannot change the color of a single hair.

5:37 "Also do not swear by the memory of a person or a thing, because all are temporary.

5:38 "Let your speech at all times simply be: Yes, yes or no, no. Anything beyond that goes against the laws.

5:39 "You have heard that it was said, an eye for an eye, and a tooth for a tooth.

5:40 "But I say to you: Exercise justice according to the natural law of Creation, so that you find the verdict in logic.

5:41 "Offer your love wherever it is warranted, and punish wherever the law of nature demands punishment.

5:42 "Give to them who ask of you, if they make their requests in honesty, and turn away from them who want to borrow from you in a dishonest way.

5:43 "You have heard that it was said, you shall love your neighbor and hate your enemy.

5:44 "However, I say to you: Exercise love and understanding according to the natural law of Creation, so that in logic you find the right behavior and feeling.

5:45 "Offer your love where it is warranted, and non approval where the law of nature demands it.

5:46 "You should be wise and learn knowledge, because you will become perfect in spirit like Creation, which conceived you.

5:47 "You should train your spirit and your consciousness in the course of incarnations and let them become perfect, so that you become one with Creation."

Chapter 6

Alms, Fasting, Treasures, Caring

6:1 “Take care regarding your piety, that you practice it before the people with correct words, lest you be accused of lying, thereby finding no reward from them.

6:2 “Choose your words using simple logic, and draw upon the knowledge and behavior of nature.

6:3 “When you give alms, you should not proclaim it, as do the hypocrites in the synagogues and on the streets, that they may be praised by the people; truly, I say to you: They have forfeited their reward, because their alms serve only their selfishness.

6:4 When you pray, you should not be like the hypocrites, who enjoy standing and praying in the synagogues and on the corners of the streets only for the sake of their selfishness and to be seen by the people.

6:5 “When you pray, you should call upon the omnipotence of the spirit and not babble like the idol worshippers, the ignorant and selfish, because they think they are heard when they use many words.

6:6 “The human spirit does not need many words, however it needs knowledge to be powerful.

6:7 “Pray therefore to the omnipotence of the spirit, in the knowledge that its greatness and power are infinite.

6:8 “If you do not know how to pray directly to the almighty power of the spirit, make use of something which is sacred to you to help you make connection to the spirit.

6:9 “But never be like the ignorant, the hypocrites, the idol worshippers and the selfish, who worship something sacred in the belief that the omnipotence of the spirit dwells in it.

6:10 "Be aware also, that through this sacred thing the almighty power of the spirit always dwells within yourself.

6:11 "Therefore pray as one who knows, and thus pray as follows:

6:12a "'My spirit, you are omnipotent.

6:12b "'Your name be holy.

6:13a "'Let your kingdom incarnate itself in me.

6:13b "'Let your power unfold itself within me, on Earth and in the heavens.

6:14-15 "'Give me today my daily bread, so that I may know gratitude and truth.

6:16a "'And lead me not into temptation and confusion, but deliver me from error.

6:16b "'For yours is the kingdom within me and the power and the knowledge forever. Amen.'

6:17 "When you pray to your spirit, it will respond to your request; trust knowledge, and you will receive.

6:18 "However, if you believe in the false teachings that the power and spirit do not dwell within you, then you will be without knowledge and will live in spiritual poverty.

6:19a "Though you will also receive now and then what you in your false belief request from misused sacred things, idols and gods, you will be receiving only out of your strong false belief, without knowledge of the real truth.

6:19b "Truly, I say to you: Blessed are only those who serve the actual truth and knowledge, because only they receive in honesty.

6:20a "When you fast, you should not look sour like the hypocrites, because they put on scowls so that their fasting will be noticed by the people.

6:20b "Truly, I say to you: They forfeit their reward therein, because they fast only for the self-seeking sake of appearances.

6:21-22 "But when you fast, anoint your head and wash your face, that you do not appear before the people with your fasting, but before your own spirit, which is hidden.

6:23 "You fast for the sake of your health and for the expansion of your spirit and knowledge.

6:24 "Neither should you amass great treasures on Earth, where moths and rust consume them and thieves break in and steal them.

6:25 "But collect treasures in the spirit and in consciousness, where neither moths nor rust consumes them and where thieves neither break in nor steal.

6:26 "For where your treasure is, there your heart is also; and the true treasure is wisdom and knowledge.

6:27a "The eye is the light of your body.

6:27b "If your eye is clear, your whole body will be light.

6:28a "But if your eye is evil, your whole body will be dark.

6:28b "If the light within you is dark, how great will the darkness be!

6:29a "No one can serve two masters: either he will hate the one and love the other, or he will adhere to the one and despise the other.

6:29b "You cannot serve your spirit and mammon.

6:30a "Therefore, I say to you: Be concerned about the knowledge of your spirit, food and drink, your body and your clothes.

6:30b "For are not the spirit, life and body more important than all the treasures of the world?

6:31 "Without the body, the human spirit, which is thirsting for truth and knowledge, is incapable of preserving its earthly life, because body and spirit are one.

6:32 "Thus you should be concerned about increasing the knowledge of your spirit, about the laws of life and about food, drink and clothing for your body.

6:33a "Look at the birds in the sky: They do not sow, they do not reap, they do not gather into barns, and yet Creation feeds them.

6:33b "Are you not much more than they?

6:34a "Look at the birds in the sky: They wipe out the harmful insects, and they have plumage for clothing, yet they have no spirit.

6:34b "They work because they carry out their duty, and they are fed and clothed by Creation.

6:34c "Are you not much more than they?

6:35 "You can think independently through your free consciousness, you can work independently and you can independently prepare food and drink and clothe your bodies.

6:36 "Behold the lilies in the marsh as they grow; they neither toil nor spin, yet truly, I say to you: The lilies also fulfill their mission, when they give pleasure to the eye with their beauty.

6:37 "I tell you, even Solomon in all his splendor was not arrayed as one of these.

6:38 "Creation nourishes and clothes the grass in the field, which today is living and tomorrow is thrown into the stove; should you then not do much more for yourselves?

6:39 "The grass fulfills its mission by serving as fodder and fuel; but are you not of much more value than grass, oh you of little faith?

6:40a "Therefore, you should care for the wisdom and knowledge of your spirit, and take care that you do not suffer from lack of food, drink and clothing.

6:40b "Truly, I say unto you: If you suffer from hunger, thirst and nakedness, then wisdom and knowledge will be crowded out by worry.

6:41 First seek the realm of your spirit and its knowledge, and then seek to comfort your body with food, drink and clothing.

6:42a "Therefore, take care for the next day, for tomorrow will not take care of you by itself.

6:42b "It is enough that each day has its own cares, so that you should not have to worry about your physical welfare."

Chapter 7

The Spirit of Judgement

7:1 "Judge not falsely, lest you be falsely judged.

7:2 "For with whatever judgment you judge, you will be judged, and with whatever measure you measure, you will be measured.

7:3 "Judge according to the logic of the laws of nature, which are from Creation, because only they possess truth and accuracy.

7:4 "Why do you see the splinter in your brother's eye and are not aware of the beam in your own eye?

7:5 "Or, how can you say to your brother: Wait, I will take the splinter out of your eye? And behold, there is a beam in your eye.

7:6 "You hypocrites, first take the beam out of your own eye, then see how you can take the splinter out of your brother's eye.

7:7 "Learn first the laws of nature and of Creation, their logic, before you condemn and pass judgment and desire to see the mistakes of your neighbor.

7:8 "Learn first through the laws of nature and of Creation to recognize your own mistakes, so that you can then correct the mistakes of your neighbors.

7:9 "You should not give sacred things to the dogs, nor throw your pearls before the swine, lest they trample them with their feet and turn on you and tear you apart.

7:10 For truly, I say to you: "Do not throw your spiritual treasure into the dirt and do not waste it on the unworthy, because they will not thank you and will tear you apart, for their understanding is small and their spirit is weak.

The Hearing of the Prayer

7:11 "Ask, and it will be given to you; seek and you will find; knock, and it will be opened to you.

7:12 "For those who ask of their spirits, receive; and those who seek through the power of their spirits, find; and those who knock at the door of their spirits, to them it will be opened.

7:13 "Which man among you would hand his son a stone if he asks for bread?

7:14 "Or offer him a snake if he asks for a fish?

7:15 So if you, now, though being wicked, can nevertheless give your children good gifts, how much more will your spirit give you, if you ask for it.

The Will of the Spirit

7:16a "Everything that you wish people would do to you, do likewise to them.

7:16b "This is the law as spoken by the prophets.

7:17a "Enter through the narrow portal.

7:17b "The portal and path leading to condemnation are wide, and there are many who travel that route.

7:18 "The portal and the way leading to life and to knowledge are narrow, and there are only a few who find it.

7:19 "Beware of false prophets and scribes, who come to you in sheep's clothing but inwardly are like ravenous wolves, preaching to you humility before shrines, false deities and gods, and preaching submissiveness to idols and false teachings.

7:20 "Beware of those who forbid you access to wisdom and knowledge, for they speak to you only to attain power over you and to seize your goods and belongings.

7:21a "You will know them by their fruits.

7:21b “Can one gather grapes from the thorns, or figs from the thistles?

7:22 “Every good seed brings forth a good harvest, but a rotten seed brings forth a bad harvest.

7:23 “A good tree cannot bear bad fruit, and a bad tree cannot bear good fruit.

7:24 “Therefore, by their fruit you will know them.

7:25 “Therefore, whoever hears these words of mine and acts upon them will be like an intelligent man who built his house on the rock.

7:26 “When a heavy rain fell and the waters came and winds blew and beat upon the house, still it did not fall, because it had been founded on rock.

7:27 “Whoever hears these words and does not act upon them is like a foolish man who built his house on sand.

7:28 “When a downpour came and flooding occurred, and the winds blew and beat upon the house, it collapsed, and it was a great fall.”

7:29 And it happened that after Jmmanuel had finished his talk, the people were shocked over his teachings.

7:30 He taught with authority a new doctrine unlike that of their scribes.

Chapter 8

The Healing of a Leper

8:1 When he went down from the mountain, many people followed him.

8:2 Behold, a leper came and knelt before him, saying, "Master, if you will, you can make me clean."

8:3 Jmmanuel stretched out his hand and touched him, saying, "I will do it. Be cleansed," and immediately he was cleansed of his leprosy.

8:4 Jmmanuel spoke to him, "See to it that you tell no one. Instead, go and present yourself to the priest.

8:5 "You were healed through the power of the spirit and the wisdom of knowledge."

The Captain of Capernaum

8:6 When Jmmanuel went to Capernaum, a centurion walked up to him with a request, saying,

8:7 "Master, my servant lies at home incapacitated with gout and is in great distress.

8:8 "Master, I have heard your new teachings and I know the truth of your wisdom, which says that the human spirit can perform miracles through knowledge of the truth."

8:9 Jmmanuel spoke to him, "I will come and make him well."

8:10 The centurion answered, "Master, I am not worthy to have you enter under my roof, but only say the word and my servant will be well.

8:11 "I am also a man subject to authority, and I also have soldiers under me; and if I say to one 'Go' he goes, and to another 'Come here,' he comes; and to my servant 'Do this,' he does it."

8:12 When Jmmanuel heard this, he marveled and spoke to those who followed him, "Truly, I say to you: Such trust I have found in no one in Israel.

8:13 "But I say to you: Many will come from the East and the West, from the South and the North, and they will understand my teaching and recognize its wisdom in knowledge.

8:14 "However, the children of Israel will be expelled into darkness; there will be wailing and chattering of teeth.

8:15 "The false teachings of Israel will bring bloodshed over the millennia, because the power-hungry selfishness and self-glorification of Israel will bring death and destruction over the land and all the world.

8:16 "Turn away from the false teachings of the Israelite authorities and their scribes, because they will bring destruction to generations of human races.

8:17 "Israel believes itself to be the chosen human race; by no means, because they are more faithless and ignorant than the heathen, who lack the secret of the laws."

8:18 Jmmanuel spoke to the centurion, "Go, be it done for you as you have believed," and his servant became well the same hour.

Jmmanuel in the House of Peter

8:19 Jmmanuel came to Peter's house and saw that his mother-in-law lay sick with a fever.

8:20 He touched her hand, the fever left her and she got up and served him.

8:21 In the evening, however, they brought to him many who were possessed; and he drove out the evil spirits through his word and made all the sick well.

8:22 So it happened that what was said through the prophet Isaiah would be fulfilled, who spoke, "He brought us new teachings of knowledge and took our infirmities upon himself, and he healed our sick."

The Seriousness of Succession

8:23 When Jmmanuel saw many people around him, he gave orders to go across to the other side.

8:24 A scribe walked up to him and spoke, "Master, I will follow you wherever you go."

8:25 Jmmanuel spoke to him, "Foxes have hollows and birds of the air have nests, but I have no fixed place where I can lay my head.

8:26 "I have the mission to preach wisdom and knowledge, therefore I am moving through the lands, restless."

8:27 One of his disciples spoke to him, "Master, permit me to go and bury my father who just died."

8:28 But Jmmanuel said to him, "Follow me and let the dead bury their dead."

The Healing of the Possessed

8:29 He came to the other side, to the country of the Gadarenes. There, two possessed persons ran up to him; they came out of the burial caves and were very dangerous, so that no one could walk on this street.

8:30a And behold, they cried out, saying, "What do you want of us, you son of Gabriel, the celestial son?

8:30b "Have you come to torment us before it is time?"

8:31 Then the evil spirits in the possessed asked him, "Master, please drive us out, so that we may go into the herd of swine grazing over there."

8:32a And he spoke, "Go there."

8:32b Then they went out into the swine, and behold, the whole herd rushed down to the water and drowned.

8:33 The swineherds fled, going into the town and telling everything, including what had happened to the possessed.

8:34a And behold, the whole town came out towards Jmmanuel.

8:34b And when they saw him, they asked him to leave their area.

Chapter 9

The Healing of the Man with the Gout

9:1 Then he stepped into the boat, went back across again and came to his town.

9:2 And behold, they brought him a man suffering from gout, lying on a bed. When Jmmanuel saw their trust, he spoke to the man with gout, "Be comforted, because your trust in the power of my spirit and in my teaching of wisdom, which is the teaching of nature and Creation, has helped you."

9:3 Behold, some of the scribes stirred up talk among the people, "This man blasphemes God and our holy teachings."

9:4 But since Jmmanuel understood their thoughts, he spoke, "Why do you think such evil thoughts against your better knowledge?

9:5 "Yet, what is easier, to say: 'Your belief has helped you,' or: 'Stand up and walk?'

9:6 "So that you may know that I am a person like you and yet know how to use the power of my spirit through my knowledge, I command the man with the gout: 'Get up, pick up your bed, and go home.'"

9:7 And he stood up, took up his bed, and went home.

9:8 When the people saw that, they were afraid and praised the amazing new teaching of Jmmanuel, which gave such power to the people.

Matthew

9:9 As Jmmanuel left there, he saw a man named Matthew sitting at the tax office. He spoke to him: "Follow me!" and he rose and followed him.

9:10 It happened, as he sat at a table in a house, behold, many tax collectors, ignorant people and seekers of the truth came and sat down at the table with Jmmanuel and his disciples.

9:11 When the Pharisees saw that, they spoke to his disciples, "Why is your master eating with the tax collectors and the ignorant?"

9:12 When Jmmanuel heard that, he spoke, "The healthy do not need a physician, but the sick do, and the knowledgeable do not need the teachings, but the ignorant do, and those who were not falsely taught do not need the teaching, but those who were falsely taught do.

9:13 "Go and recognize the falseness of your wrong teachings, so you don't mislead those people who thirst for the truth."

Fasting

9:14 Then the disciples of John came to him, saying, "Master, why do we and the Pharisees fast and you and your disciples do not fast?"

9:15 Jmmanuel said to them, "How can the ignorant fast and suffer while they are being taught knowledge?

9:16 "And how can the teacher fast, if he has to teach knowledge to the ignorant?

9:17 "Truly, I say to you: Your teachings are false if you fast according to the laws of a cult; fasting serves only the health of the body and the growth of the spirit.

9:18 "No one mends an old garment with a new patch of cloth, because the patch will tear off again from the garment, and the rip will become worse.

9:19 "Neither is new wine poured into old wineskins, or the skins will tear and the wine spill, and the wineskins will be ruined. Instead, new wine is put into new wineskins, so they are both preserved."

The Daughter of Jarius
The Women with the Issue of Blood

9:20 While he was talking with them, behold, one of the rulers of the community came and knelt before him, saying, "My daughter has just died, but come and lay your hand on her so she will live."

9:21 And Jmmanuel stood up and, with his disciples, followed him.

9:22 Behold, a woman who had hemophilia for twelve years stepped up behind him and touched the fringe of his garment.

9:23 She spoke to herself, "If only I could touch his garment, I would be cured."

9:24 Then Jmmanuel turned around and saw her, saying, "Be comforted, your confidence has helped you." And the woman was well from that hour on.

9:25 When he came to the ruler's house and saw the fife players and the turmoil of the people, he spoke,

9:26 "Depart, because the girl is not dead but is asleep." And they laughed at him.

9:27 However, when the people had been driven outside, he went in and took her by the hand, saying, "I order you, get up and walk."

9:28 And the young girl got up and walked, and soon the news of this spread throughout the whole land.

The Blind Man and the Two Mutes

9:29 As Jmmanuel went on from there, a blind man followed him, crying, "Oh Lord, you son of wisdom and knowledge who can use the power of your spirit, take pity on me."

9:30 When he came to the house, the blind man stepped up to him, and Jmmanuel spoke to him, "Do you have confidence that I can do this?" and he said to him, "Yes, master."

9:31 Then he touched his eyes, saying, "Be it done to you according to your faith."

9:32 And his eyes were opened and he saw.

9:33 Then Jmmanuel warned him, saying, "See to it that no one learns what happened to you."

9:34 However, the man went out and spread the news of him throughout that whole country.

9:35 After the man had left, behold, they brought him two people who were mute and possessed.

9:36a The mutes spoke after the evil spirits had been driven out.

9:36b And the people were amazed, saying, "Such things have never been seen in Israel; how mighty is this new teaching about the power of the spirit, that it can accomplish such miracles."

9:37 However, the Pharisees spoke, "He drives out the evil spirits through their chief, and he blasphemes God, our Lord."

9:38a And among themselves they spoke, "Who is this Jmmanuel, who possesses greater wisdom and greater knowledge than we!

9:38b "His teachings are mightier and more correct than ours, so he endangers us.

9:38c "We must try to seize him, so that he will suffer death."

The Great Harvest

9:39 Jmmanuel went about in all the cities and villages, teaching in their synagogues and preaching the secret of Creation and of the laws of nature, so that the spirit would attain omnipotence.

9:40 He preached about the spiritual kingdom within people and healed all sickness and infirmities.

9:41 When he saw the people he took pity on them, because they were languid and scattered like a herd of sheep with no shepherd.

9:42 Then he spoke to his disciples, "The harvest is great, but few are the laborers to bring it in.

9:43 "Seek and pray in your consciousness that more laborers will be found for the harvest."

9:44 So it happened that workers for the harvest were found; they gathered around the disciples of Jmmanuel.

Chapter 10

The Calling of the Disciples

10:1 He called his twelve disciples to him and gave them the knowledge to control the unclean spirits, so they could drive them out and heal all sickness and infirmities.

10:2 The names of the twelve disciples are these: Simon, called Peter, and Andrew, his brother; James, the son of Zebedee, and John, his brother;

10:3 Phillip and Bartholomew; Thomas and Matthew, the tax collector; James, the son of Alphaeus, and Thaddeus;

10:4 Simon Canaaeus, and Judas Iscariot, the only one besides Jmmanuel who understood handwriting.

10:5 Jmmanuel sent out these twelve, commanding them and saying, "Do not go into the streets of Israel, and do not go to the scribes and Pharisees, but go to the cities of the Samaritans and to the ignorant in all parts of the world.

10:6 "Go to the unenlightened, the idol worshippers and the ignorant after I have left you, because they do not belong to the house of Israel, which will bring death and bloodshed into the world.

10:7 "Go and preach, saying, 'The laws of nature are the laws of Creation, and the power of the human spirit embodies life.'

10:8 "Heal the sick, raise the dead, cleanse the lepers, drive out evil spirits. Because you received without paying, give without pay also.

10:9 "You should not amass gold, silver or copper in your belts.

10:10 "Also, you shall not take with you any large bags in your travels with which to carry food, water and clothing.

10:11 "Go on your way with only those things necessary for eating and sleeping, keeping yourselves clean and changing clothes on your journey.

10:12 "Never carry too much with you, because you would only burden yourselves and become welcome victims of thieves.

10:13 "Remember furthermore, each piece of work is worth its pay, and if you preach diligently and teach knowledge, you will not be wanting anything.

10:14 "When you go into a city or village, inquire if someone is there who is worthy; and stay with him until you depart.

10:15 "And when you enter a house, salute it.

10:16 "If the house is worthy, your peace will come upon the occupants. But if it is not worthy, your peace will return to you.

10:17 "If someone will not take you in or listen to your words, leave that house or that city and shake the dust off your feet.

10:18 "Truly, I say to you: Do not stay in such places, because they are places of ignorance and evil; people there will not recognize the words of truth and knowledge.

10:19 "Flee from those places, because the residents are disloyal to nature, and they worship holy things, false gods and idols, but not Creation, nor do they follow its laws.

10:20 "Flee from those places, for people there will try to take your life, because they do not want to forsake their false teachings.

10:21 "Flee from the unbelieving, because you should not lose your life for the sake of truth and knowledge. No law demands that of you, nor is there one that admits to such recklessness.

10:22 "Truly, I say to you: Many will nevertheless die and shed their blood into the sand, because later my teachings will be made into false teachings that I never preached and which originate in the minds of the scribes and priests.

10:23 "Thereby they will bring the people under their control through belief in their false teachings, in order to rob them of their goods and belongings.

10:24 "In all the world there will be wailing and chattering of teeth when the blood flows from all those who have made my teachings of wisdom and knowledge into false teachings, and when the blood flows from all those who in their false belief and through malicious deception believe and advocate these false teachings—teachings that are not mine.

10:25 "Many of these false believers will lose their lives, including many Israelites, who will never find their peace until the end of the world, because they are ignorant and unwise and deny the power of the spirit, of love and of knowledge.

10:26 "Truly, I say to you: The nation of Israel was never one distinct people and has at all times lived with murder, robbery and fire. They have acquired this land through ruse and murder in abominable, predatory wars, slaughtering their best friends like wild animals.

10:27 "May the nation of Israel be cursed until the end of the world and never find its peace.

10:28 "Behold, I am sending you among the ignorant and worshippers of idols, like sheep among the wolves. Therefore be clever as serpents and innocent as doves.

10:29 But beware of the people, because they will turn you over to the courts and scourge you in their synagogues.

10:30 "And you will be led before sovereigns and kings on account of my teaching as witnesses to them and to all other ignorant people.

10:31 "If you cannot flee and they turn you over to the courts, do not worry, because the power of your spirit will not leave you, and your knowledge will tell you what you should say.

10:32 "It will not be you who speak, but the power of your spirit with its knowledge.

10:33 "You will have to be hated for the sake of my teaching. But those who persevere to the end will be great.

10:34 "And when they persecute you in one city, flee to another.

10:35 "Do not go to too much trouble with the cities of Israel, for truly, I say to you: You will not get anywhere with the people of Israel until the end of the world.

10:36 "The disciple is never above the teacher, nor the servant above the master.

10:37a "It is enough for the disciple to be like his teacher and the servant like his master.

10:37b "If they have called the master of the house Beelzebul, how much more will they malign those of his household?

10:38 “Therefore, beware of Israel, because it is like an abscess.

10:39 “However, do not be afraid of them, because there is nothing hidden that will not be revealed and nothing secret that will not be known.

10:40 “What I tell you in darkness, speak in the light; and what is whispered into your ear, proclaim from the roof tops.

10:41 “Do not be afraid of evil slander, neither fear those who take life and limb.

10:42a “Do not think that I have come to bring peace on earth.

10:42b “Truly, I have not come to bring peace, but the sword of knowledge of the power of the spirit, which dwells within the human.

10:43 “I have come to bring wisdom and knowledge and to provoke son against father, daughter against mother, daughter-in-law against mother-in-law, servant against master, citizen against government and believer against preacher and priest.

10:44 “People’s enemies will be their own family members.

10:45a “The path of truth is long and the wisdom of knowledge will penetrate only slowly.

10:45b “Dark ages will follow, centuries and millennia, before the truth of the spirit will penetrate to the people.

10:46 “The unrighteous and the ignorant, including the scribes, priests and authorities, will hate those having the knowledge, so they will persecute them and sow enmity.”

Chapter 11

The Question of the Baptist

11:1 After Jmmanuel had finished giving such commands to his twelve disciples he went on from there, teaching and preaching in their cities.

11:2 When John in prison heard about the works of Jmmanuel, he sent out his disciples to him and had them ask,

11:3 "Are you the one to come, the king of wisdom, as foretold by the prophets, or should we wait for another?"

11:4 Jmmanuel answered them, "Go back and tell John what you hear and see:

11:5 "The blind see, the lame walk, the lepers are cleansed, the deaf hear, the dead rise and the truth of knowledge is proclaimed to those who seek it.

11:6 "And blessed are those who do not take offense at my teaching."

The Testimony Regarding the Baptist

11:7a Going on from there, Jmmanuel began to speak to the people about John, "What did you go out into the wilderness to see?

11:7b "Did you expect to see a reed shaken by the wind?

11:8a "Or what did you go out to see?

11:8b "Did you expect to see a man clothed in soft raiment?

11:8c "Behold, those who wear soft raiment are in kings' houses with the rulers and the rich, and with the hypocrites, scribes and priests.

11:9a "Or what did you go out for?

11:9b "Did you expect to see a prophet?

11:9c "Yes, I tell you: He is more than a prophet.

11:10 "This is he of whom it is written, 'Behold, I will send my messenger before you, who shall prepare your way.'

11:11 "Truly, I say to you: Among all those born of women, no one has arisen who is greater than John the Baptist.

11:12 "Since the days of John the Baptist even to now, the earth has suffered from violence, and those who commit violence seize the land.

11:13 "All the prophets and the law have prophesied up to the time of John.

11:14 "And if you want to accept it, he is Elijah who will come again in his future life.

11:15 "Those who have ears, let them hear!

11:16a "To what should I compare this generation?

11:16b "It is like the children who sit at the market and call to their playmates, saying,

11:17 "'We struck up a tune for you, and you would not dance; we wailed before you, and you would not mourn.'

11:18 "John, who is Elijah, came neither eating nor drinking; so they say: 'He is possessed.'

11:19a "But I have come, eating and drinking, and so they say, 'Behold, what a glutton and winebibber the man is, a companion of tax collectors and infidels.'

11:19b "Yet wisdom is justified through the acknowledged deeds."

Praise of the Spirit and of Knowledge

11:20 At that time Jmmanuel began to speak, "Praise be to Creation, maker of the heavens and the universes and the Earth, that it has kept hidden the knowledge and power of the spirit from the unwise and unintelligent who spread the false teachings, and is now revealing it to sincere seekers.

11:21 "Yes, it has been very good of Creation, and consequently of god and his celestial sons, that they have thwarted up to now the misuse of power among the human races.

11:22 "All things have now been given over to mankind, and no one knows the secret of Creation, not even one person, and neither god nor his followers.

11:23 "And all things have now been given over to me by god, whose guardian angels taught me the laws and knowledge of nature and the laws emanating from Creation.

11:24 "So come to me, all who are seeking and are thirsty for knowledge and truth; I will refresh you.

11:25 "Take the yoke upon yourselves of having to learn the new teaching, because it is the enlightenment; in it you will find peace for your life,

11:26 "because the yoke of spiritual development is gentle, and its burden is light."

Chapter 12

Regarding Marriage and Cohabitation

12:1 It happened that Jmmanuel began to speak about the laws of marriage and related topics, and he said,

12:2 "You have been given the commandment, 'You should not commit adultery.'

12:3 "Despite this, people commit adultery and fornication, thus violating the laws of nature.

12:4 "It is also written, 'Whoever commits adultery and fornication should be punished,' because the fallible are unworthy of life and its laws, thus they should be castrated and sterilized.

12:5 "If unmarried men and unmarried women bed down with one another in disgrace and without loving each other, they should be punished also, because the fallible are unworthy of life and its laws; thus they should be castrated and sterilized.

12:6 "And if two men bed down with each other, they should also be punished, because the fallible are unworthy of life and its laws and behave heretically; thus they should be castrated, expelled and banished before the people.

12:7 "If, however, two women bed down with one another, they should not be punished, because they do not violate life and its laws, since they are not inseminating, but are bearing.

12:8 "When inseminator and inseminator join together, life is violated and destroyed, but if conceiver and conceiver get together there is neither violation nor destruction nor procreation.

12:9 "Truly, I say to you: There are no animals under the sky that are like people and would go against the laws of Creation and nature; but are you not much more than the animals?

12:10 "No animal under the sky can be found whereby male cohabits with male, or female with female, because both male and female animals follow the laws of nature.

12:11 "A person who indulges in fornication for the sake of pay or pleasure should be castrated or sterilized, expelled and banished before the people.

12:12 "A person who sexually abuses a child is unworthy of life and its laws and should also be punished with loss of life, castration or sterilization, in order to be deprived of life's freedom forever and live in bondage and isolation.

12:13 "A person who indulges in incest is unworthy of life and its laws and should also be punished by loss of life, castration or sterilization, and be deprived of life's freedom forever and live in bondage and isolation.

12:14 "A person who cohabits with an animal is unworthy of life and its laws and should be castrated or sterilized, expelled and banished before the people.

12:15 "A person who marries a man or woman divorced in guilt should be castrated or sterilized, because he or she is unworthy of life and its laws, and they should both be expelled and banished before the people.

12:16 "A person who begets a child without being married to the woman is unworthy of life and its laws and should also be punished by castration and loss of his life.

12:17 "A person who rapes a woman or a man is unworthy of life and its laws and shall be punished by castration or sterilization, so that he forfeits his freedom and lives in bondage and isolation forever.

12:18 "A person who commits violence to another person, be it physically or by killing or assaulting his thinking, is unworthy of life and its laws and shall also be punished, so that he will be deprived of his freedom as long as he lives and spend his life in bondage and isolation.

12:19 "Truly, truly, I say to you: These laws of order were given by nature and should be followed, or human beings will bring death to themselves and to the masses.

12:20 "This earth can nourish and support five hundred million people of all the human races. But if these laws are not followed, in two thousand years ten times five hundred million people will exist, and the earth will not be able to support them any more.

12:21 "Famines, catastrophes, world wars and epidemics will control the earth, and the human races will commit suicide, with only a few surviving.

12:22 "Truly, I say to you: There will be wailing and chattering of teeth when so much human blood is shed upon the sands of the earth that new life forms will arise from it, which will bring the final horror to mankind.

12:23 "But on this day you have been allowed to receive all good things, and the laws have been given to you by which you should live.

12:24 "And you should adhere to additional laws, so that you will have prosperity on earth and peace in your families.

12:25 "Do away with the enforcement of the old law that woman should be subject to man, since she is a person like a man, with equal rights and obligations.

12:26 "But when a man marries a woman, he should pay to her most trusted steward of her possessions a price as security, so that she will not suffer from lack of necessities.

12:27 "The price should everywhere and always be reckoned such that a hundred pieces of silver will be required for each year of the woman's age, if her health is not lacking. Thus she will be measured in accordance with her knowledge, abilities and strength.

12:28 "The price should not be considered that of a purchase, but as security for the woman, so that she will not suffer any lack.

12:29 "The bond of matrimony between man and woman should be permitted only if both are mentally competent and capable of conducting a marriage according to the laws.

12:30 "A marriage agreement between man and woman should be concluded only when the price for the woman is paid.

12:31 "If, according to prearranged agreement, no price is paid, the law applies that the man must provide for all the wife's necessities.

12:32 "A wife's infertility is no cause for divorce, nor for other judgment or action.

12:33 "The only basis ever for divorce, besides adultery, is the destruction or endangerment of the material consciousness, the body, or the life of a member of one's own family.

12:34 “A person who is divorced with guilt should be sterilized, expelled and banished before the people, because he is unworthy of life and its laws.

12:35 “If all is done and adhered to in this way, justice and peace will come to all human races and life will be preserved.”

Chapter 13

Jmmanuel and the Sabbath Day

13:1 At that time Jmmanuel walked through a field of grain on the Sabbath; and his disciples, being hungry, began to pluck ears of grain and to eat.

13:2 When the Pharisees saw that, they spoke to him, "Behold, your disciples are doing what is not allowed on the Sabbath."

13:3 But he spoke to them, "Have you not read what David did when he and those with him were hungry?

13:4 "How he went into the temple and ate the bread of the Presence, which neither he nor they were supposed to eat, but only the priests?

13:5 "Or have you not read in the law, how on the Sabbath the priests in the temple violate the Sabbath and yet are without guilt?

13:6 "Truly, I say to you, you generation of vipers: A stone will turn into bread before no work may be done on the Sabbath.

13:7 "For the law that the Sabbath be kept holy is only a man-made law without logic, as are all man-made laws that contradict the laws of Creation.

13:8 "False prophets and distorters of the scriptures are the guilty ones responsible for these false laws that contradict the laws of Creation and of nature.

13:9 "It is a human law that the Sabbath be holy and no one work on that day, but that law is one of false teaching emanating from the human mind, and it escapes logic.

13:10 "Truly, I say to you: No Sabbath is holy and no law dictates that on the Sabbath no work may be done.

13:11 "Thus the Sabbath is a day like any other day when the day's work may be done.

13:12 "Humans have a will of their own, thus they alone are masters over the Sabbath, as was written in those old scriptures and laws that were not adulterated by false prophets and distorters and Pharisees."

13:13 He went on from there and came into their synagogue where he continued to teach the people.

13:14 And behold, there was a man with a withered hand, and they asked him, "Is it lawful to heal on the Sabbath?" in order that they would have a stronger case against him.

13:15 But he spoke to them, "You hypocrites, if only you had eyes, ears and comprehension, so that you could see, hear and understand; but you are blind and without understanding, because you lack the knowledge to see, hear and understand nature, and you also lack appreciation of the laws of Creation so that you could see, hear and understand that Creation does not keep the Sabbath holy.

13:18 "Every Sabbath day Creation turns the stars in the sky, regulates the sun, winds and rains and nourishes all creatures on earth.

13:19 "Creation causes the waters to run in their channels, and everything goes its usual way on one Sabbath as on another, as it was formed by Creation.

13:20 "But are not people much more than all the creatures and plants? They are masters over them all, if they follow the true laws!

13:21 "You generation of vipers, you scripture distorters who spread false teachings because of your greed for money and power, who among you who has a single sheep that falls into a pit on the Sabbath day, would not take hold of it and pull it out?

13:22 "How much more is a person worth than a sheep or your deceitful and false teachings!"

13:23a Then he spoke to the man, "Stretch out your hand!"

13:23b And he stretched it out; and it was sound again, like the other hand.

13:24 Then the Pharisees went out and held counsel about him, as to how to destroy him, since he made known their lies and false teachings before the people.

13:25 When Jmmanuel learned of that, he withdrew from there; and many followed him, including many sick people, and he healed them all.

13:26 He threatened them not to spread the news about him, because he was afraid that he would be captured and die the death of a martyr.

13:27 But his determination to spread the truth prevailed, so he continued to reveal his teachings and wisdom to the people.

Chapter 14

The Offense of Judas Iscariot

14:1 It happened that Jmmanuel and his disciples went to Bethlehem where he taught and advised the people.

14:2 However, Judas Iscariot had become disloyal to the teachings of Jmmanuel and lived only for his desires.

14:3 Secretly he was collecting from Jmmanuel's audiences and accumulating gold, silver and copper in his money bag so he could live oppulantly.

14:4 And it happened that Juda Ihariot, the son of Simeon, the Pharisee, informed Jmmanuel of the wrongdoings of Judas Iscariot, since he hoped to be paid for this.

14:5 But Jmmanuel thanked him and did not pay him with any gifts whatever, so Juda Ihariot thought of revenge, because he was greedy for gold, silver and copper.

14:6 But Judas Iscariot was led into the desert by Jmmanuel where, for three days and three nights, he was taught by him the concept of right and wrong, so the disciple repented and forthwith followed the teaching of Jmmanuel.

14:7 When he returned to the city, he distributed all his possessions and collections among the poor and became a trusted disciple of Jmmanuel.

14:8 However, at the same time it happened that the writings in which Judas Iscariot had reported on the teaching of Jmmanuel were stolen from him; so he told Jmmanuel about it.

14:9 And he spoke, "Truly, truly, I say to you, Judas Iscariot: You will have to suffer even greater evils than only the loss of your writings about my teachings and my life.

14:10 "For over two thousand years you will be wrongly accused of betraying me, because Simeon the Pharisee wants it so.

14:11 "But his son, Juda Ihariot, is the real culprit; like his father, Simeon Ihariot, he is a Pharisee who is seeking my life.

14:12 "It is he who stole the writings from you and brought them to the scribes and Pharisees, so they can judge me accordingly and put me to death.

14:13 "He received seventy pieces of silver for your writings and will receive another thirty when he makes it possible to deliver me over to the executers.

14:14 "Truly, I say to you: He will certainly succeed at that, and for two thousand years you will innocently have to pay the penalty for that, so you will become a martyr.

14:15 "But write down my teaching and life story one more time, because the time will come, in two thousand years, when your writings will be revealed.

14:16 "Until then my teaching will be falsified and will become an evil sect, for which reason much blood will flow,

14:17 "because the people are still not ready to comprehend my teaching and to recognize the truth.

14:18 "Not until two thousand years will an insignificant man come who will recognize my teaching as truth and spread it with great courage.

14:19 "He will be vilified by the resulting sects and advocates of the false teachings about me and be considered a liar.

14:20 "And you, Judas Iscariot, will until then be innocently reviled as my betrayer and thus be condemned, as a result of the deceit of the chief priests and the ignorance of the people.

14:21 "But pay no attention, because the teaching of truth demands sacrifice that must be made.

14:22 "In their spirit, consciousness and knowledge the people are still not very great, so they must first bring upon themselves much guilt and error before they learn thereby to accumulate knowledge and wisdom so that they can recognize truth.

14:23 "Write down my teaching and life story one more time so that all this will happen and the knowledge of truth in people will bring forth a rich harvest; thus my teachings will be handed down to posterity and bear fruits of the truth.

14:24 "Stay with me from now on, follow me and faithfully carry out your duty as the writer of my teaching, which is also the teaching of the laws of nature and thus the original laws of Creation.

14:25 "Never will there be a will greater than the will of Creation, which reveals itself through the laws.

14:26 "However, the laws of Creation are valid for yesterday, today, tomorrow, the day after tomorrow and for all time.

14:27 "Thus do the laws both determine and also predetermine things of the future that must happen."

Chapter 15

The Meaning of the Parables

15:1 That same day Jmmanuel went out and walked to the sea, where he sat down.

15:2 Many people gathered around him, so that he stepped into a boat and sat down, and all the people stood on the shore.

15:3 He talked to them in parables about various things, saying, "Behold, a sower went out to sow.

15:4 "And while he sowed, some seeds fell on the pathway; then the birds came and ate them up.

15:5 "And some fell on the rocks, where there was not much soil.

15:6 "And as the sun rose high, they withered, and because they had no roots, they dried out.

15:7 "Some fell among the thorns; and the thorns grew up and smothered them.

15:8 "Some fell on good ground and bore fruit, some hundredfold, some sixtyfold, some thirtyfold.

15:9 "Those who have ears, let them hear."

15:10 The disciples stepped up to him and said, "Why do you give your teachings to them in parables, when they do not understand them?"

15:11 He answered, "It has been given to you to understand the secrets of the spirit, but it has not been given to them.

15:12 "They certainly hear my words, but they still live and think according to the false teachings of their scribes and Pharisees.

15:13 "Their consciousness is unknowing and empty, so they must first learn to think.

15:14 "What would be better to make them come alive and think, if not by speaking in parables!

15:15 "Truly, I say to you: Life and the knowledge of truth are only valuable and good when they are obtained through one's own thinking or through the solving of secrets provided by parables.

15:16 "The human being still has little knowledge and is without insight, and the laws of Creation and the power of the spirit are not yet a reality to mankind.

15:17-18 "First, mankind must learn to recognize the truth and thus to live according to the laws of Creation so as to become knowledgeable and mighty in spirit.

15:19 "For those who have, to them will more be given, so that they have abundance; but those who have not, from them will be taken what they have.

15:20 "Therefore I speak to them in parables, because with seeing eyes they do not see, and with hearing ears they do not hear; nor do they understand.

15:21 "And in them the prophecy of Isaiah is fulfilled that says: 'With your ears you will hear and will not understand; and with seeing eyes you will see and not perceive.'

15:22 "For these people are hardened in their hearts, the ears of these human beings hear poorly and their eyes slumber, so that they will not see with their eyes, hear with their ears, understand with their minds, or comprehend the truth and the laws given by Creation, thereby attaining help and knowledge.

15:23 "For the people of Israel are unfaithful to the laws of Creation and are accursed and will never find peace.

15:24 "Their blood will be shed, because they constantly commit outrages against the laws of Creation.

15:25 "They presume themselves above all the human races as a chosen nation and thus as a separate race.

15:26 "What an evil error and what evil presumption, for inasmuch as Israel never was a nation or a race, so it was never a chosen race.

15:27 "Unfaithful to the laws of Creation, Israel is a mass of people with an inglorious past, characterized by murder and arson.

15:28 "Only few fathers in the masses of these unfaithful have an honorable past and a traceable family tree.

15:29 "These, however, do not belong to the generation of vipers who have pledged themselves to the false Judaic faith,

15:30 "to the false beliefs and false teachings that they took over from Moses who in turn stole them from the Egyptians.

15:31 "These few patriarchs are knowers of truth and true knowledge, and they recognize only the laws of Creation.

15:32 "However, they have become rare in this land and can be counted on one hand.

15:33 "They are only a few, and no one's eyes may see them, and no one's ears may hear them.

15:34 "But blessed are your eyes, that they see and your ears, that they hear.

15:35 "Truly, I say to you: Many prophets and righteous men have wanted to see what you see but did not see it and to hear what you hear but did not hear it.

15:36 "So listen now to the secret of this parable about the sower:

15:37 "If someone hears words of truth about the spirit or the laws and does not understand them, the evil one comes and snatches away what was sown in his mind; those were the seeds that were sown on the pathway.

15:38 "The seeds that were sown on the rocks are the ones who hear the word and immediately take it up with joy,

15:39 "but they have no roots in themselves, so that the seeds could firmly grow. They are fickle and take offense when misery and persecution arise on account of truthfulness.

15:40 "The seeds that were sown among the thorns are the ones who hear the word, but the cares of the world and the deception of material riches smother truth and knowledge, and they bring forth no fruit.

15:41 "The seeds that were sown on good ground are the ones who accept the word and seek and find the truth, so they can live according to the laws of truth. Thus they allow the fruit to grow and ripen, which brings forth a rich harvest; one person bears a hundredfold, another sixtyfold and another thirtyfold.

15:42 "These are the meanings of the parables, whose secrets must be deciphered by the people, in order that they learn to think and develop insights.

15:43 "Nevertheless, the path towards finding wisdom and truth is long. Compliance with the laws of Creation is also long, yet the laws are so obvious."

The Weeds among the Good Fruit

15:44 He put before them another parable, saying, "The spiritual kingdom is like a man who planted good seeds in his field.

15:45 "But when he slept, his enemy came and sowed weeds among the good seeds and went away.

15:46 "When the plantings grew and bore fruit, the weeds also appeared.

15:47 "Then the servants came to the sower and said, 'Master, did you not sow good seed in your field? Where have the weeds come from?'

15:48 "He spoke to them, 'An enemy did this.' Then the servants said, 'Do you want us to go out and pull up the weeds?'

15:49 "But he said, 'No, lest you uproot the good fruit at the same time.

15:50 "'Let both grow together until the harvest, and around harvest time I will tell the reapers: First gather the weeds and bind them in bundles that they may be burned and the ashes strewn over the field so that the soil will be nourished; but gather the good fruit and stack it for me in my barn.'

15:51 "For behold," said Jmmanuel, "both grow side by side, the weeds and the good fruit.

15:52 "The weeds hinder the good fruit from growing, yet later the weeds will become compost and nourish the ground.

15:53 "Were it not for the weeds being made into nourishment for the soil, the good fruit could not grow since it needs nourishment."

The Mustard Seed

15:54 He presented the people with another parable, saying, "The spiritual kingdom is like a mustard seed that a man took and sowed in his field.

15:55 "It is the smallest among the seeds, but when it is grown, it is bigger than all the shrubs and becomes a tree, so that the birds come from the sky and dwell in its branches."

The Leaven

15:56 He told the people another parable, "The spiritual kingdom is like leaven, which a woman took and mixed into three bushels of flour until it was thoroughly leavened."

15:57 Jmmanuel told the people all this in parables, and he did not talk to them without using parables,

15:58 so that it would be fulfilled what was spoken through the prophet, who says, "He will open his mouth in parables and will proclaim what has been hidden since the beginning of the world." This was so that people could learn thereby, find the truth and recognize and follow the laws.

The Treasure in the Field and the Precious Pearl

15:59 "Those who have ears, let them hear: The spiritual kingdom is like a hidden treasure in the field, which a man finds and conceals; and in his joy over it he goes out and sells everything he has and buys the field.

15:60 "Once more, the spiritual kingdom is like a merchant who searched for fine pearls. When he found a precious pearl, he went and sold everything that he had and bought it.

15:61 "Again, the spiritual kingdom is like a net that was thrown into the sea and caught all kinds of fish.

15:62 "When it was full, the fishermen pulled it ashore, sat down, sorted the good fish into containers but threw the useless ones away.

15:63 "Such is the spiritual kingdom, which rules within humans and whose ruler is the human being.

15:64 "Accordingly, pay heed to the parables and learn to solve their secrets, so that you learn to think and recognize and follow the laws of Creation.

15:65 "Have you understood all this?" And they said, "Yes."

15:66 Then he said, "Therefore, every scribe who has become a disciple of the spiritual knowledge and the spiritual kingdom is like the father of a household who brings out of his treasure the new and the old."

The Nazareth

15:67 It happened that Jmmanuel went away from there after he had finished these parables,

15:68 and coming to his home town of Nazareth, he taught in the synagogue. The people were shocked, saying, "How did he come by such wisdom and mighty works?

15:69a "Is he not the son of the carpenter, Joseph, whose wife became pregnant by the son of a guardian angel?

15:69b "Is not his mother named Mary?

15:69c "Are not his brothers Judas, Joseph, Simeon and Jacob?

15:70a And his sisters, are they not all with us?

15:70b "From where does he get all this wisdom and the power for his mighty works?"

15:71 So they took offense at him and threatened to turn him over to the courts.

15:72 But Jmmanuel spoke, "A prophet is never esteemed less than in his own country and in his own house, which will prove true for all the future, as long as humanity has little knowledge and is enslaved by the false teachings of the scribes and the distorters of true scripture.

15:73 "So it will prove true in two thousand years, when mankind has become knowing and thinking, that my actual unfalsified teaching will be revealed anew.

15:74 "The new prophet of that distant future will not possess so much strength and power over evil and sickness,

15:75 "but his knowledge will be above mine and his revelations about my real teaching will shake the framework of the whole earth, because at his time the world will be inundated by my teachings as falsified by the scribal distorters and will be living in a false sect that will bring death.

15:76 "It will be a time when wars from space begin to threaten, and many new gods will seek power to rule over the earth.

15:77 "Truly, truly, I say to you: The new prophet will be persecuted not only by a distrustful people, as will happen to me, but also by the whole world and by many false sects that will provide many false prophets.

15:78 "Yet, by the end of two thousand years the new prophet will reveal my unfalsified teaching to small groups, as I also teach to small groups of trusted friends and disciples the wisdom and knowledge and laws of the spirit and of Creation.

15:79 "Nevertheless, his path will be very difficult and full of obstacles, because he will begin his mission in a peace-loving country in the North, ruled by a rigid false sect based upon scriptural distortions of my teachings.

15:80 "Thus I prophesy, and thus it will be."

15:81 And there he did not show great signs of his power, and did not make known his great wisdom, because of their disdain for the truth.

Chapter 16

Herod and the Baptist

16:1 At the time that Jmmanuel dwelled in Nazareth, news about him reached Herod.

16:2 And he spoke to his people, "This surely is John the Baptist, who has arisen from the dead and therefore possesses such mighty powers."

16:3 For Herod had seized John, bound him and put him into prison because of Herodias, the wife of his brother Philippus, and had him beheaded.

16:4 It occurred that John reprimanded Herod, saying, "It is not good that you have taken Herodias, because you have committed adultery with her and you have to be punished according to the law."

16:5 He would have liked to kill the Baptist but was afraid of the people, because they considered him to be a prophet.

16:6 However, when Herod celebrated his birthday, the daughter of Herodias danced before them, which pleased Herod a lot.

16:7 Therefore he promised, with an unlawful oath, that he would give her whatever she would demand of him.

16:8 And after that she said, as she had been instructed by her mother, "Bring to me the head of John the Baptist on a silver platter."

16:9 The daughter of Herodias cried as she said it, for she loved John the Baptist, and not just because she believed in his teaching.

16:10 The king was glad that Herodias had persuaded her daughter to demand the head of John the Baptist, because this way he was not guilty in the eyes of the people, inasmuch as he had given an oath.

16:11 But Herodias' daughter did not know that Herod and her mother had agreed, even before the dance, to demand the head of John the Baptist through her.

16:12 Thus Herod sent someone and had John beheaded in prison.

16:13 His head was carried in on a silver platter and given to the young girl.

16:14 She kissed the brow of the head that had been cut off, cried bitterly and said,

16:15 "I did not know that love tastes so bitter."

16:16 Then she brought the head of the Baptist to her mother.

16:17 His disciples then came, took up the body and buried it. Then they went to Jmmanuel and told him what had happened.

16:18 When Jmmanuel heard this he was overcome with fear, and he went away on a boat to a deserted area. When the people heard that, they followed him on foot from the cities.

16:19 Jmmanuel saw the large crowd from the water. Feeling sorry for them, he went ashore and healed their sick.

The Feeding of the Five Thousand

16:20 In the evening his disciples came to him and said, "This area is so deserted and night is falling; tell the people to go away so that they can buy food and drink in the villages."

16:21 Jmmanuel said, "It is not necessary that they go away; give them something to eat and drink."

16:22 But they said, "We have nothing here but five loaves of bread and three fish."

16:23 Jmmanuel said, "Bring them to me."

16:24 Telling the people to sit down, he took the five loaves of bread and the three fish. Then he said some secret words, broke the loaves of bread and the fish and gave them to his disciples, who gave them to the people.

16:25 They all ate and were filled and saved what had been left over, twelve baskets full of morsels.

16:26 And there were about five thousand who had eaten.

Walking on the Sea

16:27 Soon Jmmanuel asked his disciples to get into the boat and to proceed without him to the city, until he could dismiss all the people.

16:28 After he had sent the people away, he climbed on a small mountain by himself so that he could rest and regain his strength. In the evening he was there by himself.

16:29 The disciples' boat was at that time in the middle of the sea and suffered a great deal because of the waves, because the wind was contrary and a storm was over them.

16:30 During the fourth night watch, Jmmanuel came towards them, walking on the waves of the sea.

16:31 When his disciples saw him walk on the water, they were terrified and said, "He is a ghost!" They were screaming with fear.

16:32 But soon Jmmanuel came nearer, spoke to them and said, "Be comforted, it is I, do not be afraid."

16:33 "Master, is it you?" Peter asked.

16:34 "Truly, it is I," said Jmmanuel.

16:35 Peter answered him, "Master, if it is you, please let me come to you on the water."

16:36 Jmmanuel said, "Come here to me and don't be afraid.

16:37 "Understand and know that the water is carrying you, and it shall carry you.

16:38 "Do not doubt your knowledge and ability, and the water will be a firm foundation."

16:39 And Peter stepped out of the boat, walked on the water and approached Jmmanuel.

16:40 But when strong thunder ripped through the howling storm, he was startled and began to sink, screaming, "Jmmanuel, help me!"

16:41 Jmmanuel quickly went to him, stretched out his hand and grabbed him, saying, "Oh you of little knowledge, why are you startled, and why do you doubt when startled?

16:42 "The power of your knowledge gives you the ability, as you have just witnessed.

16:43 "You trusted in my words before the thunder came, but then you were startled and began to doubt, and then the power of knowledge left you and your ability disappeared.

16:44 "Never doubt in the power of the spirit, which is part of Creation itself and therefore does not know any limits of power.

16:45 "Behold, there was a little bird that circled high in the sky and whistled rejoicing about life when a strong gust of wind came and made it waver. It suddenly doubted its power to fly, plummeted down and was killed.

16:46 "Therefore, never doubt the power of your spirit and never doubt your knowledge and ability, when logic proves to you the law of Creation in truth and correctness."

16:47 They stepped into the boat, and Jmmanuel commanded the storm to stop. It abated, and the winds ceased.

16:48 Those who were in the boat marvelled and said, "You are indeed a master of the spirit and someone who knows the laws of Creation.

16:49 "No one like you has ever been born, nor has any prophet known to us had such power."

16:50 But Jmmanuel answered, "I tell you there are greater masters of spiritual power than I, and they are our distant ancestors of Petale [the mental plane close to Creation].

16:51 And great are they also, those who came out of space, and the greatest among them is god, and he is the spiritual ruler of three human races.

16:52 "But above him is Creation whose laws he faithfully follows and respects; therefore he is not omnipotent, as only Creation itself can be.

16:53 "Thus there are limits for him who allows himself to be called god and who is above emperors and kings, as the word says.

16:54 "People are ignorant and immature because they consider god as Creation and follow the false teachings that were adulterated by scribal distorters.

16:55 "Thus, when people believe in god, they do not know about the truth of Creation, because god is human as we are.

16:56 "There is a difference, however, that in his consciousness and wisdom, logic and love he is a thousand times greater than we and greater than all people upon this earth.

16:57 "But he is not Creation, which is infinite and without any form.

16:58 "Thus, god is also a creature of the Creation, which, according to illogical human judgment, has no beginning and no end."

16:59 They sailed across the sea and went ashore at Gennesaret.

16:60 When the people there became aware of him they sent word all over the land and brought to him all who were sick.

16:61 They asked him if they might only touch the hem of his garment so that they would be healed.

16:62 Thus it took place; those that touched the hem of his garment became well.

Chapter 17

The Human Commandments and the Laws of the Creation

17:1 Pharisees and scribes from Jerusalem came to Jmmanuel, saying,

17:2 "Why do your disciples disregard the laws of the elders?"

17:3 He answered, "Why do you violate the laws of Creation by following your laws?

17:4 "Moses said, according to the laws of mankind, 'You must honor your father and your mother; but those who unjustly honor their father and mother shall die.'

17:5 "The teaching of the laws of Creation is this: You shall honor father and mother; a person who does not honor father and mother shall be expelled from his family and the society of the righteous.

17:6 "But you teach people to say to their father or mother, 'I sacrifice to the sect whatever is supposed to be yours, so I am free from you.'

17:7 "Therefore you wrongly teach that people no longer need to honor their father or mother. Thus you have traded the laws of Creation for your own laws and lust for power.

17:8 "You hypocrites, Isaiah prophesied about you accurately, saying,

17:9 "'The people of Israel honor Creation with their lips, but their heart and their knowledge are far from it.

17:10 "'They serve their sect in vain because they teach such falsified and deceptive beliefs, which are nothing but man-made laws.'"

17:11 And Jmmanuel called the multitude to him and said: "Listen and understand!

17:12 "The teachings of the scribes and Pharisees are wrong and falsified, because they teach you man-made laws, which are not the laws of Creation."

17:13 And his disciples came to him and said, "Do you know that the scribes and the Pharisees took objection to your word when they heard it?

17:14 "They went out to witness against you and to have you killed because of your teaching."

17:15 But he answered and spoke, "All plants that do not live according to the laws of Creation, will dry up and rot.

17:16 "Let them, because they are the blind leading the blind; but when a blind man leads another blind man, both will fall into the ditch.

17:17 "Let us go away, so that the persecutors remain without booty."

17:18 Peter said to him, "Please interpret your speech about the plants and the blind men for us."

17:19 But Jmmanuel reprimanded his disciples and said, "Are you also still without understanding and therefore ignorant and doubting in recognition, comprehension and understanding?

17:20 "You have been with me for a long time, but you still lack the ability to think and recognize the truth.

17:21 "Truly, I say to you: You yourselves will do much towards falsifying my teaching in the future.

17:22 "With your knowledge you barely exceed that of the other people.

17:23 "Haven't you realized yet that all the parables and speeches have a spiritual meaning and are therefore about the spiritual life of men?

17:24 "Oh, you of little knowledge, does your understanding still not exceed the stupidity of the people?

17:25 "Beware, or you will see me in a false light and accuse me of an origin that I cannot claim."

Chapter 18

The Pharisees Demand A Sign

18:1 Jmmanuel went away and escaped to the area of Sidon and Tyre.

18:2 And behold, the Sadducees and Pharisees came to him and demanded that he let them see a sign of his spiritual power.

18:3 But he answered, "In the evening you say, 'Tomorrow will be a fair day, because the sky is red.'

18:4 "And in the morning you say, 'Today will be foul weather, because the sky is red and cloudy.' So you can discern the appearance of the sky, but can't you then also discern the signs of the time?

18:5 "This wicked and faithless generation is seeking a sign; there shall be no sign given to it but the sign of Jonah who disappeared alive into the belly of the fish, stayed therein and came again alive into the light."

18:6 And he left them and went away.

The Leaven of the Pharissees

18:7 When they sailed across the sea and arrived ashore on the other side, they had forgotten to take bread along.

18:8 And Jmmanuel spoke to them, "Take care and beware of the leaven of the Pharisees and the Sadducees."

18:9 They spoke to each other and said, "That probably means something to the effect that we haven't taken along bread or something else to eat."

18:10 When Jmmanuel heard this, he was angry and said, "Oh you of little knowledge, why does it worry you that you have no bread?

18:11 "Don't you understand yet, and can't you have the imagination to understand my words?

18:12 "Are you of such little knowledge and without understanding that you are unable to recognize the meaning?

18:13 "Do you still not understand, and do you wish not to understand for all time to come?

18:14 "Don't you remember the five loaves of bread and the three fish divided among the five thousand and how many baskets you lifted up?

18:15 "How is it that you do not understand that I am not speaking to you about the bread that you eat every day? But I tell you this, beware of the leaven of the Pharisees and the Sadducees."

18:16 Then they finally understood that he had not said to beware of the leaven of the bread, but of the false and adulterated teachings of the scribes and Pharisees.

The Faith of Peter

18:17 Jmmanuel came into the area of Caesarea Philippi and asked his disciples, "Who do the people say that I am?"

18:18 They said, "Some say that you are John the Baptist, others that you are Elijah and others again that you are Jeremiah or one of the old prophets."

18:19 And he said to them, "But who do you say that I am?"

18:20 Simon Peter answered, "You are the prophesied Messiah and a son of the living god who is the spiritual ruler of three human races."

18:21 Jmmanuel became angry and answered him, "Oh you unfortunate one, my teaching has not revealed that to you, because I instructed you in the truth.

18:22 "And I also tell you: You certainly are a faithful disciple, but your understanding must be compared to that of a child.

18:23 "You are Peter, and I cannot build my teachings on your rock. You will open the portals of ignorance, so that people will be overcome by your false interpretation of my teaching and will follow it and live according to falsified teachings.

18:24 "I cannot give you the key of the spiritual kingdom, otherwise you would open false locks and wrong portals with it.

18:25 "I am not the son of the spiritual ruler of three human races and therefore not the son of god, and so only Creation governs the spirit, but never a human being; therefore remove yourself from this erroneous teaching and learn the truth.

18:26 "My mother is Mary who conceived me through a guardian angel, a descendant of our ancestors from out of space, and my earthly father is Joseph who only acts as a father substitute."

18:27 He threatened his disciples never to tell or wrongly assume such things and not to spread the false teaching of Peter.

The Proclamation of the Passion

18:28 From that time on, Jmmanuel began to tell his disciples that he would have to go to Jerusalem and suffer much from the elders, scribes and chief priests, because he could not help but keep his teaching from them.

18:29a Peter went up to him and angrily said to him, "May god or Creation prevent that!

18:29b "This had better not happen to you, because they will catch, torture and kill you."

18:30 He turned to Peter, became angry and said, "Get away from me, Satan, for you are an annoyance, because you are thinking not in spiritual, but in human terms.

18:31 "Simon Peter, again you make me angry and show your ignorant thinking.

18:32 "Truly, I say to you: Because of your ignorance the world will shed much blood, because you will falsify my teaching and spread it erroneously among the people.

18:33 "You will be guilty of the death of many people, the origin of a false name for me and the evil insults of calling me the son of god, and calling god Creation itself.

18:34 "But you are still under the grace of my long-suffering patience, and you can still measurably improve upon your ignorance."

18:35 Then Jmmanuel said to his disciples, "Anyone who wants to follow my teaching should take upon himself the burden of the search for truth, realization and understanding,

18:36 "because those who live their lives in truth and knowledge will be victorious, but those who live their lives in untruth and ignorance will lose.

18:37a "What would a person profit if he gained the whole world and damaged his consciousness?

18:37b Or, how can a human being help his spirit if he is unable to think?

18:38 "Truly, I say to you: There are some here who will not taste the power of spiritual knowledge in this life, which they will learn in the next life.

18:39 "The human spirit is ignorant until it has gained knowledge through thinking and inquiry.

18:40 "A person's spirit is not a machination of humanity but is a part of Creation given to him. It must be made aware and perfected,

18:41 "so that it proceeds to be one with Creation, since Creation, too, lives in constant growth.

18:42 "Creation is timeless, and so is the human spirit.

18:43 "The teaching of this knowledge is extensive and not easy, but it is the way to life, manifold in its manner.

18:44 "People's lives are destined to reach the perfection of the spirit, so that they live their lives in fulfillment thereof.

18:45 "Even if people make mistakes, they act according to a law of Creation and they learn from them and gather perception and knowledge, thereby cultivating their spirits and being able to act according to their strength.

18:46 "Without making mistakes it is impossible to gather logic, insight, knowledge and wisdom necessary to cultivate the spirit.

18:47 "Truly, I say to you: The teachings of the chief priests, Pharisees and scribes are deceptive and false when they tell you that a mistake would be punished by god or Creation, when the mistake serves the perception and knowledge and therefore the progress of the spirit.

18:48 "Just as there is no punishable mistake that serves the perception, knowledge and progress of the spirit, likewise, there is no inheritable mistake for which there is punishment in this world or another world.

18:49 "Punishment of such a mistake would contradict all the laws of nature and thus, all the laws of Creation.

18:50 "If one commits a mistake that will serve the insight and knowledge of the spirit, there is no punishment in this life or in another life.

18:51 "If people live with the mission to perfect their spirits and obtain insight and knowledge through their mistakes, they lead lives for which they were destined.

18:52 "Because a person does not learn consistently according to the greatness of his spirit, which is governed by the laws of Creation, he is led into situations that must be consequent, since they are set up. Thus, he misleads his consciousness, thinking, feeling and acting, and he heaps guilt upon himself and opens up his spirit to attacks from other people's power.

18:53 "The spiritual powers of other people affect the life of the individual, either good or bad.

18:54 "If people at this time begin to think and understand, they need the teaching; therefore, the prophets have been sent by the celestial sons to teach the human races the true laws of Creation and knowledge regarding life.

18:55 "But the people are still ignorant because they do not understand the new teaching in its truth and follow the false laws of the chief priests and distorters.

18:56 "Lacking understanding, the people curse the truth that has to come; they curse, stone, kill and crucify the prophets.

18:57 "But since the teaching of the truth has to be spread among the people, the prophets have to bear great burdens and suffering under the curse of the people.

18:58 "Just as they persecuted many prophets, they are now after my life.

18:59 "The prophecy of the inexorable destiny applies to me, that I, although innocent, will be declared guilty.

18:60 "However, I will not be killed, but being in a state of near-death, I will be considered dead for three days and nights. I will be placed in a tomb, so that the sign of Jonah will be fulfilled.

18:61 "My friends from faraway India, who are well versed in the art of healing, will be my caretakers and help me flee from the tomb on the third day, so that I will then finish my mission with people of India.

18:62 "It will happen that I will attain a certain insight, increase my knowledge and bring about a new strength in spirit and consciousness."

Chapter 19

The Thought of a Child

19:1 It happened that the disciples stepped up to Jmmanuel and said, "Who is the greatest in spirit?"

19:2 Jmmanuel called a child, placed the youth among them

19:3 and spoke, "Truly, I say to you: Unless you change and become like the children, you will not become great in spirit.

19:4 "Those who search, seek and gather understanding and thirst for knowledge like this child will be great in spirit.

19:5 "Those who search, seek and find like such a child will always reach their fullest potential within themselves.

19:6 "But they who do not heed this truth, follow false teachings and neither search nor find would be better off with a millstone hung around their necks and drowned in the deepest sea.

19:7 "Truly, there is no sense in life and no fulfilling of its meaning without searching, seeking and finding.

19:8 "It would be better to expel those who do not understand from the social life of the true seekers and of those who search for true life, so that they don't hinder those willing to seek the truth.

19:9 "But certainly the unreasonable ones will be willing to pay attention to the laws of Creation in their lives after expulsion.

19:10 "Woe to the world because of annoyances, because trouble must come through troublemakers; but woe to those by whom annoyances are caused.

19:11 "Don't worry if your hand or foot annoys you and falls off. It is better to lose a limb and to grow great in spirit than to have two hands and two feet and a spirit that remains small in consciousness or even withers.

19:12 "Don't worry if an eye troubles you and becomes blind. It is better for you to see the laws of Creation in the power of your spirit and consciousness than to have two eyes and be spiritually blind.

19:13 "See to it that you don't belong to those who are sound in body but sick and lacking in consciousness.

19:14 "Seek the meaning and truth of my teaching. Since I am human like you, I, too, had to seek and understand.

19:15 "Since I am human like you and have gathered my knowledge, you are also capable of learning, searching, understanding and knowing; in so doing you understand and follow the laws of Creation.

The Mistakes of the Fellow Men

19:16a "If your fellow man makes mistakes and embraces false teachings, go to him and confront him in private.

19:16b "If he listens to you, you have won your fellow man.

19:17 "If he does not listen and continues to misunderstand, leave him, because he is not worthy of your teaching once you've done everything possible.

19:18 "It is better to let an unreasonable person walk on the path of misery than to bring confusion to one's own spirit.

19:19 "Truly, I say to you: The heavens will fall down before an unreasonable person can be taught reason; therefore, beware of them.

19:20 "Sow the seeds of wisdom on fertile soil where they can germinate,

19:21 "because only germinated seed will bring forth fruit."

Chapter 20

Marriage, Divorce and Celibacy

20:1 After Jmmanuel had finished speaking, he departed from Galilee and came into the Judean land beyond the Jordan.

20:2 Many people followed him, and he healed the sick there.

20:3 The Pharisees came up to him, tempted him and said, "Is it right for a man to divorce his wife for any cause?"

20:4 He answered, "Truly, I say to you: Stars would sooner fall from the sky than for divorce to be permissible.

20:5 "Truly, a man will leave his father and mother for the sake of marriage and will be attached to his spouse, and they both will be one flesh and blood.

20:6 "They are no longer two, but one flesh and blood, and that union is their own.

20:7 "From one flesh and blood they bring forth offspring, who again are one flesh and blood of their father and mother.

20:8 "What has been joined together in this way, let no one put asunder, because it is against the laws of nature."

20:9 And they asked, "Why did Moses command them to issue a letter of separation in case of divorce?"

20:10 He answered them, "Moses gave you permission to divorce because of the hardness of your hearts and his dominion over you, but it has not been so since the beginning of the human races, because in this instance Moses has broken a law.

20:11 "But I say to you: Whoever divorces, except for fornication or other stipulated errors made by the other, and marries someone else, is breaking a marriage."

20:12 And the disciples said to him, "If that's the way it is between a man and his spouse, it is not good to marry."

20:13 But he spoke to them, "Not everyone understands this word, except those to whom it is given,

20:14a "for some do not enter marriage because from the time of their birth they are unsuited for it; some do not enter marriage because other people have made them unsuited for it, and still others do not enter marriage because they renounce it for the sake of spiritual strength.

20:14b "Those who can grasp this, let them grasp it."

The Blessing of the Children

20:15 Then children were brought to him, so that he would lay his hands on them and bless them, but the disciples rebuked them.

20:16 However, Jmmanuel spoke, "Leave the children alone and do not stop them from coming to me; because they are my most attentive listeners and of such is the realm of wisdom."

20:17 And he put his hands on them and said, "Learn knowledge and wisdom, and you will become spiritually perfect and true followers of the laws.

20:18 "Truly, I say to you: Inasmuch as I am called Jmmanuel, which means 'the one with godly knowledge,' you, too, shall bear this name so that you will understand the wisdom of knowledge."

20:19 He said to his disciples, "Truly, truly, I say to you: Seek knowledge and understand the truth, so that you will be wise.

20:20 "Since I am named 'the one with godly knowledge,' which means truth is among us, I stand spiritually above kings and emperors.

20:21 "Thus I am the king of wisdom among the human races, as god is the king of wisdom among the sons of heaven, who are the creators of three human races.

20:22 "As I was born by an earth woman and speak her language, I am called Jmmanuel, as god in his language is called god, which means king of wisdom, and he is often a ruler over a human race and master over the people.

20:23 "Seek and understand the meaning of my speech lest you may be so bold as to call me the son of god or the son of Creation, or to insult me by calling me the ruler over good and evil.

20:24 "Behold the little children, they are not like you; they trust in the truth and wisdom of my speech, and therefore wisdom shall be theirs. So why do you push them away?"

20:25 And he put his hands on them and departed.

20:26 As they were walking, Peter said to him, "Behold, we have forsaken everything to follow you, and what will we get in return?"

20:27 Jmmanuel replied, "Truly, I say to you: Some of you who have followed me will embrace the wisdom of my teaching, so you will be spiritually great in reincarnations to come. But some of you will misunderstand the wisdom of my teaching and spread false teachings about me. They shall have a difficult time finding the truth in coming incarnations.

20:28 "Thus it will always be among all human races everywhere from East to West, and from North to South.

20:29 "My valuable teaching will be brought to many, but they will not understand it.

20:30 "Many will follow a false teaching about me and therefore not find the truth, because they mistake me for god or his son, or perhaps even the son of Creation.

20:31 "They will speak big words and insist that they alone know the truth, because they have become victims of a terrible mistake and thus follow an evil and falsified teaching.

20:32 "Many will be first among the human races, because they will think humanely in their false teachings, but they will be last in spiritual knowledge and small in their wisdom.

20:33 "Wisdom will only exist where the knowledge about truth bears fruit and the laws of Creation are followed and respected."

Chapter 21

Two Blind Persons

21:1 When they went to Jericho, many people followed him.

21:2 And behold, two blind men sat by the wayside; and when they heard Jmmanuel going by, they cried and said, "Oh Lord, son of a celestial son, have mercy on us."

21:3 The people threatened them so that they would be quiet. But they screamed even louder and said, "Oh Lord, son of a celestial son, have mercy on us."

21:4 And Jmmanuel stood still, called them and said, "What do you want me to do for you?"

21:5 They said to him, "Lord, open our eyes so we can see the beauty of the world."

21:6 And he had pity on them and said, "What do you suppose, whose power is it that can make you see?"

21:7 They said, "The power of Creation, which is in the laws."

21:8 Jmmanuel was astonished and said, "Truly, so far I have never seen such faith and knowledge among these people. Be it done to you as you believe."

21:9 And he touched their eyes and immediately they saw and followed him.

21:10 As they went on their way Jmmanuel taught the people in candid words, saying,

21:11 "Truly, truly, I say to you: If you are knowledgeable and understanding in spirit and embrace wisdom, and if you practice love in truth and don't doubt, you will not only do such things with blind eyes, but when you say to the fig tree: Dry up, it will dry up, or when you say to a mountain: Lift yourself up and throw yourself into the sea, it will come to pass.

21:12 "Be knowledgeable in truth and wisdom, so that your spirit and your consciousness will become powerful.

21:13 "When you are knowledgeable and live in the truth of wisdom, your spirit will be filled with infinite power.

21:14 "Everything that you command or ask for in prayer, you will receive, when you believe in it.

21:15 "Do not suppose, however, that prayer is necessary, because you will also receive without prayer if your spirit is trained through wisdom.

21:16 "Do not err by paying attention to the falsified teaching that a person has a will, because this belief is wrong.

21:17 "Know then, people are obligated at all times first to create a will for whatever they want to attempt, because such is the law of nature.

21:18 "Thus they determine the course of their lives, which is called fate.

21:19 "But they must acquire knowledge and learn truth from which they create a will that follows the laws.

21:20 "Consider yourselves as people who live in order to learn and to perfect the spirit,

21:21 "because you were born with the task of becoming perfect in spirit.

21:22 "Don't worry about the future, when the false teaching is spread that people have to perfect themselves in spirit once more because they have fallen away from Creation.

21:23 "Beware of this false teaching because it is wrong to the last dot on the 'i'.

21:24 "Truly, truly, I say to you: Humanity was never perfect in spirit and so has never fallen away from Creation.

21:25 "Each person's spirit is created individually for the task of perfecting itself and to reach wisdom,

21:26 "so that it may become one with Creation according to the destiny of the laws, whereby Creation itself may grow, expand and perfect itself.

21:27 "And as the spirit in a person is a unit, so is Creation in itself a unit and has no other powers beside it.

21:28 "In itself, Creation is pure spirit and therefore infinite power, because it is one within itself, and nothing exists outside of it.

21:29 "Therefore, beware of the false and adulterated teachings of the future, which will insult me by calling me the Son of Creation and also the son of god.

21:30 "These teachings lead to lies, and because of them the world will suffer much deprivation and distress.

21:31 "Don't pay attention to the false teachings of the future, which will try to make the spirit, Creation and me into a trinity, which again is a unit.

21:32 "Beware of these false and adulterated teachings of the future, because a trinity is impossible according to the logical laws of Creation.

21:33 "Truly, I say to you: The princes keep their people down, and the sovereigns do violence to them; but the new cults also will use their power to do violence by adulterating and spreading my teachings.

21:34 "So beware of them and do not be forced to carry the yoke of false teachings.

21:35 "This should not happen to you, because you shall be great and learn and teach truth.

21:36 "As I have come to teach wisdom and knowledge among the people, so shall you continue to teach, in order that the truth may prevail."

Chapter 22

Jmmanuel's Entry into Jerusalem

22:1 When they came near Jerusalem, to Bethpage near the Mount of Olives, Jmmanuel sent out two of his disciples, and said to them,

22:2 "Go to the place ahead of you, and soon you will find a female donkey tied to a post and a foal with her; untie her and bring her to me, because she was a gift to me and is only kept there.

22:3 "If anyone asks you a question say, 'Jmmanuel of Nazareth needs her,' and immediately he will let you have her."

22:4 The disciples went there and did as Jmmanuel had told them.

22:5 They brought the female donkey and the foal, and they laid their clothes on the old animal, and he sat upon them.

22:6 When the people heard that Jmmanuel, the king of wisdom, would come, they spread their clothes on the path. Others cut off branches from the trees and spread them out on the path.

22:7 The people who went ahead of him and those who followed him shouted and said, "Hail to the descendant of David. Praise him who comes to announce the new teaching of truth."

22:8 When they entered Jerusalem, the whole city was excited and said, "Who is it that's coming?"

22:9 The people said, "That is Jmmanuel, the prophet from Nazareth in Galilee, who brings anew the teaching of truth."

The Purging of the Temple

22:10 Jmmanuel went into the temple in Jerusalem and became furious when he saw that dealers, sales people, merchants dealing with doves and money changers had established themselves there.

22:11 Jmmanuel became upset and spoke to them, "It is written: 'The temple is to be a place of teaching, a place of contemplation.' But you change it into a den for thieves."

22:12 In his anger he kicked over the tables of the money changers and the chairs of the dealers of doves and drove them all out with the whip of a donkey driver.

22:13 And the blind and lame came to him in the temple and he healed them all.

22:14 But when the chief priests and scribes saw the great deeds he accomplished and the people who were shouting in the temple, saying, "Hail to the descendant of David," they became enraged

22:15 and asked him, "Do you hear what these people are saying?" Jmmanuel said to them, "Are you so afraid of the truth that it angers you?"

22:16 He left them there, departed the city for Bethany and stayed there overnight.

Back in Jerusalem

22:17 When Jmmanuel came again into the temple and taught, the chief priests, scribes and the elders of the people came to him and demanded, "With what authority are you doing these things, and who gave it to you?"

22:18 And Jmmanuel answered them, "I too want to ask you a question, and if you answer that, I will tell you by whose authority I am doing this.

22:19a "Whence came the baptism of John? From Creation or from men?"

22:19b They pondered the question and spoke among themselves, "If we say it was through Creation, then he will reply, 'Why don't you believe in it, and why aren't you following its laws?'

22:20 "But if we say it was through men, we will have to be afraid of the people because they consider John a prophet."

22:21a So they answered Jmmanuel, saying, "We don't know."

22:21b Then he said to them, "You generation of vipers, neither will I tell you by whose authority I do these things.

22:22 "But what do you think? A man had two sons and went to the first one and said, 'My son, go and work today in the vineyard.'

22:23 "He answered, 'Yes father, I will go.' Yet he did not go.

22:24 "So he went to the other son and said, 'My son, go and work today in the vineyard.'

22:25 "But he answered and said, 'I don't want to do it and therefore I will not go.' However, he soon felt remorse and went.

22:26 "Now I ask you: Which of the two did the will of the father?" They said, "The latter, of course."

22:27 Jmmanuel spoke to them, "Truly, truly, I say to you: The publicans and prostitutes will understand the wisdom of knowledge before you do.

22:28 "John and the prophets came to you and taught you the right way and you didn't trust them; but the publicans and prostitutes trusted them. And even though you understood it, you did not repent and change your mind, so that you would have believed them from that time on.

22:29 "You know the truth, and yet you deny it, in order to profit in the use of gold, silver and goods and to get rich at the expense of the poor, who have been led astray. You mislead and exploit them in the name of the faith.

22:30 "But listen to another parable about a vineyard, and perhaps you will understand, if your mind still works.

22:31 "There was a lord who owned much. He planted a vineyard, built a fence around it and dug a cellar in it, and he built a tower, leased the vineyard to vine-dressers and left the country.

22:32 "When the time of the grape harvest arrived and with it the payment of the lease, he sent his servants to the vine-dressers, so that they would receive his loan.

22:33 "The vine-dressers seized his servants, beat one, tortured the other and stoned to death the third one.

22:34 "Again the master sent out other servants, more than the first time, and the vine-dressers treated them the same as they did the servants before.

22:35 "At last he sent the son of his administrator to them and said, 'They will be afraid of the administrator's son.'

22:36 "But when the vine-dressers saw the son of the administrator they spoke among themselves, 'This is the heir, come let us kill him and take over his inheritance.'

22:37 "They seized him, pushed him out of the vineyard and killed him, so they thought. While presuming him to be dead, they put him in a tomb where he was in a state of near- death for three days and three nights, and then he fled. Then he returned to the lord of the vineyard and reported to him.

22:38 "When the lord of the vineyard heard what had happened to the son of his administrator, what do you think he did?"

22:39 They said to him, "He probably had the villains punished and banished and turned his vineyard over to other vine-dressers who paid his lease at the right time, and he most certainly turned over the inheritance to his administrator's son earlier."

22:40 Jmmanuel spoke to them, "You recognized the meaning, and you have read it in the scriptures: 'The stone that the builders threw away became the cornerstone.'

22:41 "Therefore I tell you: I am like the son of the administrator of the vineyard, and you are like the vine-dressers that leased the vineyard.

22:42 "My teaching truly is not strange to you and is very well known, because it has already been handed down to you by the prophets through whom you know it.

22:43 "But if you disdain and falsify it to your advantage, you call me a liar, and you also call god a liar. It was upon god's advice that I was begotten by one of his kind, and because of god that I stand as a prophet before you.

22:44 "Therefore I say to you: Peace and joy shall forever be taken from you and your people and be given to a people who cultivate their fruits.

22:45 "If you disregard and trample all the laws of god who is the ruler over this and the two other human races in the North and the East, you will be scorned and trampled for all time to come.

22:46 "The burden of the Judeans will be like a heavy stone of the seven great ages, and whoever falls upon this stone will be shattered, but whomever it falls upon will be pulverized."

22:47 When the chief priests and Pharisees heard his speeches they understood that he cursed them and the people for all time to come.

22:48 They thought about how they could seize him, but they were afraid of the people who believed him to be a prophet.

Chapter 23

Tax Money

23:1 When the Pharisees held counsel as to how they could catch Jmmanuel in his speech, they sent to him their followers, including Herod's people.

23:2 Then they spoke, "Master, we know that you are truthful, teach the law properly and do not consider the rank of a person, because you do not respect people's esteem but only the laws of god and Creation.

23:3 "Therefore, tell us your opinion. Is it right to pay tax unto Caesar, or is it not?"

23:4 But Jmmanuel sensed their malice and said, "You hypocrites, of what low mentality are you to want to tempt me in such a sick manner?

23:5 "Show me a tax coin so that I can heal you from your sick stupidity." And they gave him a coin.

23:6 He said to them, "Whose image and whose inscription are on this coin?"

23:7 They replied, "They are the emperor's."

23:8 He then said to them, "Therefore, give to Caesar the things that are Caesar's, and give to god the things that are god's, and give to Creation the things that are Creation's.

23:9 "Yet beware and know that god and the emperor are people above whom is the omnipotence of Creation to which you must give the highest praise,

23:10 "for although god and the emperor are indeed rulers over the human races and the peoples, above them stands Creation as the highest power on which they depend, just as does each human being and all life."

23:11 They heard this with astonishment, left him alone and went away.

Rebirth

23:12 On the same day the Sadducees, who do not believe in rebirth, came up to him.

23:13 They asked him,"Master, Moses has said: 'When a man dies and has no children his brother shall take the widow as his wife and beget descendants for his brother.'

23:14 "Once there were seven brothers among us. The first one was married and died, and because he had no descendants he left his wife to his brother;

23:15 "and so did the second and the third, until the seventh.

23:16 "At last the woman also died.

23:17 "Now you teach there is a new life. Whose wife will she be among the seven in the new life? All of them had her as a wife."

23:18 Jmmanuel answered, "You are mistaken and don't know the unadulterated scriptures of the elders, nor do you know the laws of Creation.

23:19 "Truly, I say to you: Moses never gave that commandment but rather gave the commandment that a brother should take his brother's wife to himself in honor, so if one died the other would take care of the widow of his brother.

23:20 "How is it possible for a brother to beget descendants for his brother, since everyone's seed is different?

23:21 "In the next incarnation they all will be strangers because they will not recognize each other; therefore, no law says the wife then belongs to this one or that one.

23:22 "In each new life if people wish to marry, which is not certain, they decide for themselves whom they wish to marry.

23:23 "Take heed of the laws of Creation, which teach that in a new life people do not remember their former lives. Thus your question is superfluous.

23:24 "At this point it is only the prophets who remember former lives, since they follow the laws of Creation and therefore live in wisdom.

23:25 "But since you and the Israelite people will live in spiritual darkness for an extended period, understanding and wisdom of the spirit and of the consciousness will remain hidden from you for a long time.

23:26 "Other peoples will advance beyond you in spirit and consciousness, evolve to a high degree and follow the laws of Creation.

23:27 "Therefore, other peoples will be superior to you in spirit and gather great wisdom, so that many among them will soon be like the prophets and remember former lives.

23:28 "But you and the people of Israel shall remain poor in consciousness and therefore drift in spiritual darkness;

23:29 "and if someone incurs punishment, he shall have to endure it."

23:30 When the people heard that, they were shocked and afraid.

The Greatest Commandment

23:31 When the Pharisees heard that Jmmanuel had shut up the Sadducees, they held a meeting for deliberation.

23:32 One among them, a scribe, tested him by asking, "Jmmanuel, which is the first commandment in the law?"

23:33 Jmmanuel asked in return, "Whose law are you thinking about? Are you thinking about the law of the emperor, the law of god or the law of Creation?"

23:34 The scribe said, "I am thinking of the laws of all three."

23:35 Jmmanuel said, "The highest commandment in the law of Creation is: Achieve the wisdom of knowledge, so that you may wisely follow the laws of Creation.

23:36 "The highest command of the law of god is: You shall honor god as ruler of three human races and follow his laws, because he is their king of wisdom and a good and just counselor.

23:37 "The highest command of the laws of the emperor is: You shall be obedient to the emperor, follow his laws and give to him the tithe, because he is the ruler over the people and their guardian and protector.

23:38 "These are the noblest and greatest laws in the three categories.

23:39 "But the other law, equal to the first, is this: You shall consider only Creation as omnipotent, because it alone is constant in all things and therein everlasting.

23:40 "God and the emperor are temporal, but Creation is eternal.

23:41 "On these two commandments depend the entire law and the prophets.

23:42 "The laws of god and those of the emperor are human laws and meant to maintain law and order among people.

23:43 "But the laws of Creation are the laws of life and spirit and therefore are eternal and constant.

23:44 "Likewise immortal is a person's spirit, which is a tiny piece of Creation, for how could Creation itself ever cease to be?

23:45 "When people die, their spirits live on and leave this existence for the beyond, where they continue to gather the wisdom of knowledge.

23:46 "According to the amount of spiritual wisdom gained through the raising of their consciousness, they decide their future and return, as well as their subsequent activities.

23:47 "Since I am also a prophet and know the future, I tell you that I will return as a representative of god. Then, teaching, I will sit in judgment of all those who follow false teachings and belittle the wisdom of the spirit.

23:48 "Therefore the words of truth will be harsh and without mercy, and many a person will fly into a rage because of them.

23:49 "The harsh words of truth will be enlightening judgment and punishment for all those who live according to false teachings and degrade the wisdom of the spirit."

23:50 When the Pharisees were together, Jmmanuel asked them, "What do you think, whose son am I?"

23:51 They said, "The son of David."

23:52 He spoke to them, "How can I be the son of David, if he has been dead for a long time and I was begotten by Gabriel, the guardian angel?

23:53 "Haven't you read that David called me lord when he said,

23:54 "'The Lord said to my lord, 'Sit down at my right side so that I can place your enemies under your feet, because you are my stepson and my successor.'"

23:55 "Since David calls me lord, how can I be his son?"

23:56 No one could give him an answer, and they said secretly, "He blasphemes God and the prophets. Let's try to catch and kill him, because he endangers our position in that we will no longer be respected by the people."

Chapter 24

Against the Scribes and the Pharisees

24:1 Jmmanuel spoke to the people and the disciples, saying, "The scribes and Pharisees sit on the chairs of the prophets.

24:2 "However, refrain from doing and accepting anything they say, and neither act according to their works.

24:3 "They teach you false teachings, which they and their forefathers have falsified for their own profit.

24:4 "They contrive heavy burdens and put them upon people's shoulders, but they themselves do not want to lift a finger.

24:5 "They do all their labor in order to be seen by people and impress them.

24:6 "They enlarge their prayer belts as well as the tassels on their clothing.

24:7 "They love to sit at the heads of tables and in the best places in the synagogues.

24:8 "And they love to be greeted at the marketplace and to be called master by the people.

24:9 "But don't let anyone call you master until you have understood the wisdom of knowledge.

24:10 "And don't let anyone call you teacher until you follow the laws of Creation,

24:11 "because those who allow themselves to be called master and teacher and do not possess the wisdom of knowledge will be denounced as liars,

24:12 "and those who undeservedly exalt themselves will be abased, and those who undeservedly abase themselves will be disdained.

24:13 "Let those who are great in consciousness consider themselves great, and those who are small in consciousness consider themselves small and those who are in between in consciousness consider themselves in between.

24:14 "It is unwise and stupid for people to let others consider them greater or smaller than they truly are.

24:15a "Woe to you, scribes and Pharisees, you impostors, hypocrites and swindlers who block people's spiritual progress towards consciousness with your lies and false teachings.

24:15b "You will not attain progress easily, and through false teachings you keep it from those who wish to attain it.

24:16 "Woe to you, scribes and Pharisees, you impostors, hypocrites and swindlers, who devour the homes of widows and engage in long prayers for the sake of appearance, therefore, you shall stay in spiritual darkness all the longer.

24:17 "Woe to you, scribes and Pharisees, you hypocrites who pass through land and sea in order to win a fellow believer; after he has become one, you turn him into an irrational and unreasonable child who indulges in twice as many false teachings as you.

24:18 "Woe to you, you blind proponents of false teachings who say, 'A person is not bound if he swears by the temple, but he is bound if he swears by the gold on the temple.'

24:19 "You fools and blind people, you are the offspring of evil; why do you let people swear, knowing that an oath is not binding and is a worthless act?

24:20 "Or you say, 'if a person swears by the altar, that does not count; but if a person swears through sacrifice, that is binding.'

24:21a "You blind and false teachers, who gave you the right to demand an oath or to swear, since the laws of Creation state that oaths should not be taken?

24:21b "Your speech should always be only 'yes, yes' or 'no, no.'

24:22a "Those who swear by anything on earth or in the universe swear by something fleeting, which is without permanence.

24:22b "Therefore, an oath is also without permanence.

24:23 "But those who swear by Creation or its laws swear by something over which they have no power. Therefore, an oath is of no consequence either.

24:24 "Therefore, those who swear by anything commit an offense with respect to the truth of their promises and make them doubtful.

24:25 "Woe to you, scribes and Pharisees, you hypocrites who tithe mint, meramie, dill and caraway seeds and neglect the most important things in the law, namely, justice, freedom of knowledge, and the truth of Creation, and you let go unnoticed the laws of love, logic and justice.

24:26a "Woe to you, you blind leaders of a hoard of blind, who say: 'This should be done and that should not be left undone.'

24:26b "You only represent a false teaching and ignore the laws of Creation.

24:27 "You blind leaders, you are flies and swallow camels that you cannot digest.

24:28 "Woe to you, scribes and Pharisees, you hypocrites who keep cups and bowls outwardly clean, yet inside they are full of rapaciousness and greed.

24:29 "You blind ones, you scribes and Pharisees, you hypocrites and distorters of the truth, first clean what is inside the cup so that it may become as clean as the outside and light up in its brilliance.

24:30 "Woe to you, scribes and Pharisees, you hypocrites who are like whitewashed tombs that appear beautiful on the outside, but inside they are full of stench, bones and filth.

24:31 "So you, too, appear pious and good in front of people, but inside you are full of hypocrisy, falsehood and violations.

24:32 "Woe to you, scribes and Pharisees, you hypocrites who build monuments for the prophets and decorate the graves of the just and say,

24:33 "'If we had lived at the time of our forefathers and fathers, we would not have become guilty with them in the shedding of the prophets' blood.'

24:34 "Woe to you, scribes and Pharisees, you impostors, hypocrites and swindlers, who secretly call the dead people of high and of common standing, so you deceive yourselves and wrongly believe to speak with them and delude yourselves.

24:35 "You cannot talk with dead people, and even if you could, the dead could tell you only the wrong thoughts they already had during their lifetime.

24:36 "You are not great enough to call upon the dead who have wisdom and can tell the truth.

24:37 "You give witness to yourselves, that you are the children of those who killed the prophets and falsified their teachings.

24:38 "Well then, you are following the way of your fathers; therefore you are ending your lives without understanding, and you will have trouble learning in the future.

24:39 "You brood of snakes and vipers, how can you be great in spirit without having any understanding?

24:40 "All the just blood that was shed through you on earth will come back to you, beginning with the first prophet your fathers and forefathers murdered, to the blood of Zacharias, the son of Barachias, whom you killed between the temple and the altar, and all the blood you cause to be shed in the future.

24:41 "You will be outcast among the human races, and then you will alternately lose your occupied land, regain it and lose it again until the distant future.

24:42 "Truly, I say to you: your existence will be continual struggle and war, and so the human races will strike you with their hostile thinking and enmity.

24:43 "You will find neither rest nor peace in the country stolen by your ancestors by means of falsehood and deceit, because you will be haunted by your inherited burden of murder with which your forefathers killed the ancient inhabitants of this continent and deprived them of life and property.

24:44 "So all the just blood will come upon you, blood which was shed by your forefathers and through you, and which is still being shed by you and your close and distant descendants until the faraway future.

24:45 "There will be hatred against you in this world, and even the future will bring you neither rest nor peace until you retreat from the land stolen by you, or until you make a conciliatory peace and create brotherly trust and unity with your enemies and renounce your false and stolen rights.

24:46 "You brood of snakes and vipers, this will happen to you into the distant future, yet not by accident you then will also have a fortunate experience when my teaching of Creation, rights and laws will again be spread, so that you may then seize the opportunity to end and settle the world's hatred against you by means of an honest peace.

24:47 "Therefore, in the future, heed my teaching, which is truly the teaching of laws and commandments of Creation; pay attention when it will be newly taught, because it will be the sign of the time at which many things change, and the power of the mighty and tyrants will break apart, so that nationalities of all human races will become free.

24:48 "In the distant future, heed the renewed presentation of my teaching of the spiritual and creative forces and laws and commandments. It is valid for all times and universal, and you will be able to act according to my counsel, and there will be quiet and peace among you and all human beings in this world.

24:49 "Truly, truly, I say to you: All this will be fulfilled and shall come upon you and upon your race and continue long into the future, as I have told you."

Chapter 25

The Prophecy

25:1 And Jmmanuel walked out of the temple, and his disciples came up to him because they wanted to show him the outside of the building.

25:2 He spoke to them, "Look at all this. Truly, I say to you: Not one stone here will remain upon the other without being broken.

25:3 "The Judeans trespass against life and truth, and they built this city on the blood of people; but these people are divided into Israelites who call themselves sons and daughters of Zion, to whom I am not close and who want to kill me, and into Judeans, who are misled believers of their sect, and to whom I bring the teachings of truth, as I do to all human races.

25:4 "The Israelites have plundered this land through rapaciousness and murder, they have killed their friends with whom they had drunk wine, and they have deceived and misled their fellow-believers of the Judean sect, who are actually Israelites but only followers of a sect.

25:5 "Thus the Israelites betrayed their own friends and murdered them because of their greed, but it will likewise happen to them on the part of the rightful owners of this land whom they have deprived of their rights and subjugated since ancient times."

25:6 And when he sat on the Mount of Olives his disciples came up to him and said, "Tell us, when will this happen, and what will be the sign?"

25:7 Jmmanuel answered, "Two thousand and more years will pass, but in the meantime Israel will never find peace because many wars and much evil threaten the unlawful owners of this land; but see to it that nobody will lead you astray.

25:8 "Many impostors and false prophets will come in my name and say, 'I am Jmmanuel, and I am the sign of the time,' and they will mislead many.

25:9 “People will hear much about wars and war cries and they shall see this but not be frightened, because this must happen; but it is not the end yet.

25:10 “Because many a nation will rise against its government, one nation against another, and one kingdom against another, there will be times of great need, earthquakes and tremendous floods all about.

25:11 “All this is the beginning of enormous calamities.

25:12a “Soon the people with the knowledge will be exposed to distress and be killed.

25:12b “They will be hated for the sake of truth in their teaching and wisdom.

25:13 “Many kinds of sects will rise up against one other, and much blood will flow.

25:14 “Then many will succumb to the attacks, and betray and hate one another because they remained small in spirit.

25:15 “Love will grow cold in many people because lack of faith will take over.

25:16 “Hatred will rule over all the world and evil will reign,

25:17 “but those who persist in the truth will survive.

25:18 “This lesson will be preached in the new age throughout the world as testimony for all peoples, and then the end will come.

25:19 “When the people see the horror of destruction in Jerusalem, of which the prophets have spoken, the end will come.

25:20 “Whoever is in the land plundered by the Israelites at that time should flee to the mountains.

25:21 “Those who are on the roof should not climb down to get anything from their houses.

25:22 “Those who are in the fields should not go back to get their coats.

25:23 “Woe to the women who are pregnant and those who are nursing their babies at that time, because they will suffer much grief and death. And there will be many of them.

25:24 “There will soon be greater grief than there has ever been since the beginning of the world, and never will there be such grief again.

25:25 "If these days were not shortened, no one would remain alive; but the days will be shortened for the sake of the spirit and of life.

25:26 "This is for the sake of people who serve the truth and the laws.

25:27 "There will be howling and chattering of teeth when this time comes, because of people's lack of understanding and greed.

25:28 "They will build machines made from metal for use in the air, on the water and on land, to kill off one another.

25:29 "They will throw heavy projectiles out of these machines made of metal, across the land and the cities,

25:30 "and fire will come out of these projectiles and burn the world so that not much will be spared.

25:31 "They will put the cornerstones of life into the projectiles to kindle the deadly fire.

25:32 "If at that time powerful people did not appear as did the celestial sons long ago, in order to bring to a standstill the unobstructed madness of the deluded dictators, truly, I am telling you: No human being would survive.

25:33 "Since the human races will at that time comprise far more than ten times five hundred million people, great parts of them will be eradicated and killed.

25:34 "This is what the law ordains, because people have violated it and will violate it again into the distant future.

25:35 "When at that point someone will say to the people, 'Behold, here is Jmmanuel, who is the sign of the time,' they should not accept it to be true.

25:36 "Because many a false Jmmanuel and many impostors and false prophets will rise and do great signs, it becomes possible to lead astray not only those who seek, believe and err, but also the scholars and intelligent people.

25:37 "Behold, I told you so before, and so it will fulfill itself.

25:38 "Therefore, when impostors and those led astray will say, 'He is in the desert,' people shall not go there, and when they say, 'Truly, he is in a chamber,' they shall not accept it as the truth.

25:39 "Since I will certainly return at that time, I will let them recognize me.

25:40 "This is how the law and destiny want it, and that's the way it will be.

25:41 "Just as lightning starts from its rise and radiates until its setting, so will be my coming in the future, when I bring the teaching anew and announce the legions of the celestial sons, when I will have a renewed life and will again be accused of deception and blasphemy over the breadth of the world, until the teaching of truth will bring about insight and change in people.

25:42 "People of all times, beware: where the carcass is, there the vultures will gather, so watch out.

25:43 "Soon after the grief of that time, sun and moon will lose their luster, comets will fall from the sky and the powers of the heavens will start to sway.

25:44 "The structure of the heavens and of the air will be disturbed, and the land will burn because of the black oil of the earth, ignited by the greed of the people, and the sky will be dark because of smoke and fire, and so the weather will break down, and severe cold and many deaths among people, plants and animals all over the earth will result from people's power senselessly developed, and people will live with their greed for power and mania and vice.

25:45 "Then there will appear signs in the sky, and all races on earth will cry and come to see the signs in the clouds of the sky that witness of great power and strict judgments against irrationality.

25:46 "Since god is the ruler over three human races, the laws and commandments of Creation will be valid in all eternity through which, as representation of Creation and human irrationality, people will judge themselves with anger.

25:47 "People owe their existence to god, who is the ruler over them, so that they have to follow his commandments and respect him as the greatest king of wisdom.

25:48 "He will send his guardian angels with loud trumpets that will gather his followers from all directions, from one end of the earth to the other.

25:49 "Do learn a parable from the fig tree; when its branch puts forth leaves, you know that summer is near.

25:50 "So it will also be at that time when the people see all of this, they will know that the end is close at hand.

25:51a "Truly, truly, I say to you: This is how it will be.

25:51b "This human race will not perish until all of this has come about.

25:52 "The heavens and the earth will pass, and so will the universe; but my words will not pass, because they are words of truth within the laws of Creation.

25:53 "No one knows the day or hour when all this will happen, neither the guardian angels, nor god himself, nor I, Jmmanuel, but only providence and destiny through the laws and commandments of Creation, which possesses the greatest wisdom.

25:54 "Creation alone rises far above all human races, and it alone deserves honor and praise, just as it renders honor and praise to the absolute power above it.

25:55 "If people revere and honor god and recognize only Creation as the supreme power, they act according to the truth."

Chapter 26

Commandments and Love

26:1 "Since the laws and commandments of Creation and the laws of god apply, they shall be followed and respected.

26:2 "Just as the laws and commandments of Creation are the laws and commandments of the spirit and of life, so the laws and commandments of god are the laws and commandments of the material and human order.

26:3 "God issued the laws and commandments both as material and human order for that which is right and also as a guideline for life.

26:4 "Thus laws and commandments serve as paths upon which humanity should walk in wisdom and intelligence so as to be righteous.

26:5 "Insofar as the laws and commandments of Creation and god are followed there is no need for people to bring forth other laws and commandments whatsoever.

26:6 "The laws and commandments of Creation and god shall be considered as the true laws and commandments and shall be followed, because they alone have consistent validity and correctness.

26:7 "If people deviate from these laws and commandments, they bring forth illogical and inadequate human laws based on false logic.

26:8 "If they are fainthearted in spirit, so are their laws fainthearted and resemble heresy.

26:9 "If they are presumptuous and disregard the laws and commandments of Creation and those of god, they are forced to bring forth their own laws, however, which are full of mistakes and lead everyone astray.

26:10 "Man-made laws and commandments always produce murder and evil everywhere, and evil will spread and prevail, and people no longer will have any control over it.

26:11 “Commandments and laws are valid only if they are derived from wisdom and logic,

26:12 “but logic requires wisdom and understanding.

26:13 “Human laws and commandments are powerless if not based upon the laws and commandments of Creation, and god’s laws and commandments, issued by him in wisdom, also rest upon the laws and commandments of Creation.

Proverbs

26:14 “Truly, I say to you: Wisdom has to be learned from the laws of Creation, which people recognize in nature.

26:15 “But if they do not think and search, they will not attain wisdom and remain fools.

26:16 “The wise do not cry over lost things, over the dead and over things of the past.

26:17 “Fools cry over things that are not worth crying over, thereby increasing their grief, need and misery.

26:18 “Those who are rich in wisdom and live according to the laws do not allow creatures to suffer even the least hurt, if they are without fault.

26:19 “Fools who do not conquer their senses mistake damage for advantage, advantage for damage and great suffering for joy.

26:20 “Because people do not follow wisdom and do not seek knowledge, nor understand the laws, they are filled with imprudence and vice.

26:21 “The dishonest, stupid, defiant, greedy, unscrupulous, uncouth and angry will be hurt like people who are poor in consciousness.

26:22 “If people receive daily in due manner just a little wisdom in their consciousness, they grow like the waxing moon during the light half of the month.

26:23 “Wisdom is the greatest asset of humanity and so is the created will, which is lord over love and happiness, but all this is meaningless without the power of the spirit.

26:24 “Fools who wait for fate to act without doing anything themselves perish like an unfired pot in water.

26:25 "Those who take care of a cow always receive milk; likewise, those who nurture wisdom and apply it through the power of the spirit bring forth rich fruit.

26:26 "Understand each law of Creation and once you have understood it, adhere to it and live accordingly, because the laws are the greatest wisdom.

26:27 "There is no eye equal to wisdom, no darkness equal to ignorance, no power equal to the power of the spirit, and no terror equal to poverty of consciousness.

26:28 "There is no higher happiness than wisdom, no better friend than knowledge, and no other savior than the power of the spirit.

26:29 "Those who have intelligence may grasp my speech so they will be wise and knowing."

The False Doctrine of Saul

26:30 When Jmmanuel had finished that speech, behold, a man named Saul came to him and said,

26:31 "You preach a new teaching, and it is strange to me from the beginning; it seems dumb to me, and your mind seems confused."

26:32 But Jmmanuel said, "How can you tell me that I am confused in mind when it is you who are confused in mind?

26:33 "Truly, I say to you: Since you are Saul and persecute me and my disciples because of my teaching, you will change your mind.

26:34 "From now on, you shall be named Paul. You will travel in all directions and will have to suffer for having called my teaching false and my spirit confused.

26:35 "You will heap great guilt upon your shoulders, because you will misunderstand my teaching and preach it falsely due to your lack of understanding.

26:36 "Your speech will be confused, and people all over the world will lapse into slavery and worship the false doctrine.

26:37 "When you place the land of the Greeks in bondage to an evil sect with your false teaching, you will call me "the anointed" in their language.

26:38 "It will be due to your ignorance that they will call me Jesus Christ, which means "the anointed."

26:39 "Because of this name so much human blood will be shed that it cannot be held in all the existing containers, which will be the fault of your ignorance.

26:40 "You are still persecuting me and my disciples because of my teaching, but soon the time will come when you will change your mind,

26:41 "when you face me again and assume that I am a ghost.

26:42 "Truly, I say to you: Like so many others, you will be greatly to blame that my teaching is adulterated and that the human races build false sects.

26:43 "You will be the cornerstone for the folly that I will be called 'Jesus Christ' and the redeemer of a false sect."

26:44 Jmmanuel was furious, seized a stick and chased Saul away.

26:45 Saul, his thoughts full of revenge, joined up with Juda Ihariot, the son of the Pharisee, and discussed how to seize Jmmanuel to turn him over to the authorities.

Suicide

26:46 When Saul had left, Jmmanuel called his disciples together, and said to them, "You know when Passover comes in two days, I shall be turned over to the courts to be crucified, as it is destined, so that I may continue to learn.

26:47 "My traitor will be Juda Ihariot, the son of Simeon, the Pharisee, because he is interested only in gold, silver, goods and chattels.

26:48 "He will betray me for thirty pieces of silver, because he is misled by his father's greed.

26:49 "But his joy in the pieces of silver will not last long, because he is fickle and unstable and will soon feel guilty.

26:50 "Since Juda Ihariot is without courage and has little knowledge, he will put his belt around his neck and hang himself from a branch.

26:51 "Truly, truly, I say to you: Although Juda Ihariot's suicide appears just, it is unjust.

26:52 "Even though people have free will to demand their rights and govern themselves, they do not have the right to decide over their lives or deaths.

26:53 "The intent of the laws is such that people live their lives to the end so that they may perfect their spirits in this manner.

26:54 "But if they judge themselves through suicide, they deviate from the law and violate the plan and the laws of Creation.

26:55 "Understand that they have no right to decide over their own lives and deaths.

26:56 "They have only the right to determine the kind of life they want to live, but not the right to decide over life and death.

26:57-58 "The laws say that no event or situation justifies suicide, and this includes suicide carried out by other persons such as hired murderers or mercy killers.

26:59 "No matter how much guilt people may incur, or how large their burden may be, they have no right to determine their own deaths.

26:60 "Even though Juda Ihariot incurs great guilt, he has no right to decide over his life and death.

26:61 "Any guilt or mistake leads to understanding and the perfection of the spirit.

26:62 "But if people escape from guilt or a mistake by suicide, they flee from understanding and responsibility and have to learn the same in another life.

26:63 "Thereby the process of perfection of the consciousness and of the spirit is delayed, which is not the will of Creation.

26:64 "Either way, suicide is an act of deplorable cowardice and a callous disregard of the laws and commandments of Creation."

Chapter 27

The Agitation of the Disciples

27:1 After Jmmanuel had finished speaking, the disciples were very excited and said, "Why don't we catch Juda Ihariot and stone him so he can't betray you?"

27:2 But Jmmanuel was furious and said, "Don't you know that the law says, 'You shall not kill in immorality?', and don't you know what I prophesied to you, that I would be crucified in order to attain a certain knowledge?

27:3 "How dare you disregard the destiny of the laws, since this is given and intended!

27:4 "As I go my way, so all people will have to go their ways.

27:5 "Truly, I say to you: If I were not to follow my destiny, how could I fulfill my mission, which will lead me to India?

27:6 "Oh, you who lack courage and knowledge, I taught you the truth and you do not recognize it.

27:7 "How can it still be incomprehensible to you that after my departure my teaching will be adulterated by you and spread as false doctrines and sects in all directions?

27:8 "So you will do, that the world will resound in false guidance and teachings.

27:9 "Many among you will bear the guilt for humanity, not recognizing the truth even though I have taught it to you.

27:10 "There will be great reverberations in the world regarding your false teachings, which you will spread.

27:11 "Namely, you did not understand the words of knowledge and the truth of my teaching.

27:12 "You and the people are struck with blindness, just like the legitimate people of this land who are held in darkness and oppression, as the prophets predicted for this human race, because the people have abandoned the teaching of truth, just like the Israelites who plundered this land and have dominated and oppressed the legitimate owners of the land.

27:13-14 "I fulfilled my mission among this generation but could not teach any reason to the people, because of the fault and false teachings of the Israelites and because they do not think reasonably because of confusing and deceptive teachings against reason; therefore, I will leave, because the teaching of the truth shall be brought also to two other human races in the North and East.

27:15 "Just as these people, who are the legitimate owners of the land under powerful Israelite rule, stand under the leadership of god, so also the other two peoples stand under him, namely, the race in the high North, where cold and ice reign on the highest mountains and at the end of the earth, and the race in the land of India, because he, god, is the master over these three human races.

27:16 "As a prophet, I have come back into the world from the realm of Arahat Athersata [a highly evolved group of spiritual guardians], sent here by god's will, so that I should teach the three human races the newly brought teaching of truth.

27:17 "Therefore, I must walk in the path that was destined by Arahat Athersata and requested by god, since I also serve his will and laws, as god himself serves the laws of Creation."

In Bethany

27:18 Jmmanuel finished speaking and left for Bethany and the house of Simon, the leper.

27:19 Behold, a woman came up to him, who had a glass of precious water, which she poured on his head as he sat at the table.

27:20 When his disciples saw that, they became angry and disturbed and said, "What is this waste good for?

27:21 "This water could have been sold at a high price and the proceeds used for the poor."

27:22a But when Jmmanuel heard this, he scolded his disciples and said, "Why are you upset by the woman?

27:22b "She did a good deed to me because she trusts in my teaching. In this way she shows her gratitude, and nothing is too expensive for her.

27:23 "This woman has become wise and lives according to the laws of Creation. Therefore she thanks me with the precious water.

27:24 "Her gratitude will be lasting, and from now on her deed shall be known throughout the world.

27:25 "Truly, I say to you: Wherever my teaching will be preached in all the world, whether falsified or true, people will remember what she has done.

27:26 "Just as she will be remembered for a long time, so a false teaching about which one of you betrayed me will also be remembered.

27:27 "While we are here together, Juda Ihariot, the son of the Pharisee in Jerusalem, is hatching a plot against me as to how he can betray me to the chief priests.

27:28 "While we are gathered here, he is asking the chief priests for the blood money that they offer for my capture.

27:29 "Thirty pieces of silver are offered to him if they catch me through his help.

27:30 "While they are forging this plan, they are also hatching the plot against one among you, since they want to present a culprit to the people.

27:31 "Thus Juda Ihariot, the son of the Pharisee, will turn me over to the soldiers, and my disciple, Judas Iscariot, is supposed to be considered the traitor,

27:32 "So that the people will say, 'Behold, these confused people are divided among themselves and therefore one betrays the other. So, how can the teaching of Jmmanuel be the truth?'

27:33 "But since Juda Ihariot, the son of the Pharisee, and my disciple, Judas Iscariot, have almost identical names, the lie of the chief priests will be accepted from the beginning."

The Last Supper

27:34 On the first day of the Unleavened Bread, Jmmanuel spoke to his disciples, "Go into the city to a good friend of mine named Aaron and say to him, 'Jmmanuel says to you: I want to have a last meal with my disciples at your house, for behold, the Feast of the Passover is near.'"

27:35 The disciples did as Jmmanuel had told them, and they prepared the meal, together with Aaron and his wife, in their house.

27:36 When they sat down and ate, he said, "Behold, the time is near when I will have to take my heavy burden upon myself.

27:37-38 "But I go only where I am supposed to go according to the prophets; however, I will only seem to be dead and suffer much pain, so you do not have to be afraid or worried about me.

27:39 "Truly, I say to you: From now on I will no longer drink of the fruit of the vineyard nor eat of the bread until I drink and eat again with you after my affliction.

27:40 "I shall lie in the tomb for three days and three nights and then rise from near-death."

27:41 When they ate, Jmmanuel took the bread, broke it, and gave it to the disciples, saying, "Take and eat; the body needs nourishment also in times of need and grief."

27:42 And he took the cup, gave it to them, and said, "All of you drink from this cup; your throats are thirsty on rainy and cold days, too.

27:43 "Truly, I say to you: A wise person does not hunger and thirst because of things that have to happen.

27:44 "But a fool hungers and thirsts through lack of understanding and anger against things that have to come about.

27:45-46 "Truly, I say to you: Just as you do not understand my words now and are angry with me because of them, so will you be angry with me tonight, because your minds still have not been enlightened.

27:47 "But when I apparently rise from the dead, from my near-death out of the tomb, I will walk in front of you to Galilee, so that you may recognize the truth of my words.

27:48 “I have taught you knowledge and truth, but you doubt and don’t trust me.

27:49 “Oh you who are fainthearted and of little trust, how startled and confused you will be, when I meet you again after having appeared to be dead.”

27:50 But Peter answered him, “Even if they all were angry with you, I would never be angry.”

27:51 However, Jmmanuel replied, “Truly, I say to you: You are one of the worst, because tonight before the rooster crows you will deny me three times.”

27:52 But Peter contradicted him, saying, “This will never come about, and even if I had to die with you, I would never deny you.”

27:53 All of his disciples agreed and did not trust the words of Jmmanuel.

Chapter 28

In Gethsemane

28:1 When they left the house of Aaron and his wife in Jerusalem, Jmmanuel went with his disciples to a courtyard called Gethsemane, which belonged to a man named Joshua, who thought well of Jmmanuel.

28:2 In the large garden of the farm he spoke to his disciples, "Sit down here while I go over there and have a chance to ponder."

28:3 He took with him Peter and the two sons of Zebedee and started to mourn and think, because he was afraid and alarmed about what would happen to him.

28:4 And he spoke to them, "Behold, certainly I am wise and have great knowledge, but I am afraid of things to come, both known and unknown. However, this is the nature of a human, even though he is knowing and wise.

28:5 "My mind is grieved to death; therefore, stay with me and watch with me, so that I do not feel so lonesome.

28:6 "It is easier to bear a hardship with one or two other persons than by oneself.

28:7 "If destiny wanted it to, this cup would pass me by, but not my will but destiny's be done, because this is what has been planned for me."

28:8 When he spoke thus, Judas Iscariot joined them and said, "Listen to what I have to say. Over there things are taking place in the shadow of the city walls, where I just noticed covered lights."

28:9 Jmmanuel said, "These are probably the henchmen that Juda Ihariot is bringing, because he has secretly followed us here in order to betray me."

28:10 He walked away, fell on his face and reflected, saying, "If it is possible, may this cup pass me by, not according to my will, but may the law of destiny be fulfilled, so that I will be enlightened in this secret, which I must fathom."

28:11 Returning to his disciples he found them sleeping and so he said to Peter, "Can't you watch with me for one hour, so I'm not alone in my difficult hour?

28:12 "Be awake and great in spirit and in consciousness so that you will not be tempted: The spirit is willing but the flesh is weak!"

28:13 A second time he walked, fell on his face and said, "If it isn't possible for this cup to pass me by, I will drink it, so that I may be enlightened in this secret and fulfill for all time my mission in a faraway country."

28:14 He returned and found the disciples sleeping again, and only Judas Iscariot stayed awake with him.

28:15 He walked away again, fell on his face a third time, brooded in bitterness and said, "I am so afraid even though I know that I have to follow my path which is destined for me.

28:16 "How willing is the spirit and how weak is the flesh when it is so frightened of pain!"

28:17 His body trembled, and fine drops of sweaty blood flowed all over him because he was so afraid and anxious.

28:18 With his face flushed, he came back to his disciples and said to them, "Do you want to sleep or rest now, or do you want to watch with me? Behold, the hour has come that I will be turned over to the hands of the henchmen.

28:19 "So get up and let us go; for behold, the henchmen are coming."

The Capture

28:20 As he was still talking, behold, there came Juda Ihariot, the son of the Pharisee, and with him a great number of chief priests and elders of the people, carrying swords and poles.

28:21 Juda Ihariot had given them a sign and said, "Behold, I will flatter him and confuse him as if I repented the sins of my life.

28:22 "And as a sign of false flattery there will be a kiss; and behold, you shall seize whomever I kiss."

28:23 He then stepped up to Jmmanuel and said, "I greet you, Master. Now I will follow your teaching, since you allow me to repent my old life."

28:24 Then he touched Jmmanuel and gave him the kiss of treason.

28:25 But Jmmanuel said to him, "My friend, why have you come to tell me a lie, when treason burns in your mind and in your actions?"

28:26 The henchmen came up to Jmmanuel, put their hands on him and seized him.

28:27 And behold, one of the henchmen pondered, had a quick change of mind and joined Jmmanuel, because he felt remorse.

28:28 He stretched out his hand, pulled out his sword, and hit a servant of a chief priest, cutting off his ear.

28:29 Then Jmmanuel said to the man, "Put your sword back into its sheath, because those who take a sword without need will perish by the sword.

28:30 "Or do you think that I could not have fled before your group arrived?

28:31 "But how could I fulfill my destiny if I had done so?"

28:32 And the man turned away crying, fled and was never seen again.

28:33 Then Jmmanuel talked to the henchmen, "You came here with swords and poles in order to capture me as if I were a murderer.

28:34 "It would have been easy for you to capture me in the city; daily I sat there teaching in the temple, yet you did not seize me.

28:35 "You hypocrites, you must have been afraid of the people, and therefore you come to me like thieves in darkness to throw me into prison and out of the sight of the people.

28:36 "Truly, I say to you: Darkness will be light, and everyone will talk of your deed for which you will be denounced for all time to come."

28:37 Then Simeon, the Pharisee, stood up and said, "Your sayings are stupid and full of lies; why should we be afraid of the people?

28:38 "You taught the people falsely, despised our laws and called them lies, and for that you have to suffer.

28:39 "You thought we would not catch you and bring you to trial, but you were mistaken,

28:40 "because one of your followers was not of your persuasion and betrayed you for thirty pieces of silver. And that is Judas Iscariot."

28:41 Jmmanuel answered, "Truly, I say to you: You may succeed for a long time in accusing Judas Iscariot of treason in front of the people, but the truth will come out and be known by all in the whole world,

28:42 "namely, that my traitor is not Judas Iscariot but is your son, Juda Ihariot, who bears the name of his father, the Pharisee."

28:43 Simeon, the Pharisee, was furious, stepped up and hit Jmmanuel in the face with his fist because he was afraid of his true words.

28:44 When this happened, the disciples, full of fear and discouraged, abandoned Jmmanuel and fled.

28:45 Those who had seized Jmmanuel took him to the high priest, Caiaphas, where the scribes, Pharisees, and elders of the people had gathered to pass sentence on him.

Jmmanuel Before the Highest Counsel

28:46 The chief priests and the high councilors were looking for false testimony against Jmmanuel so that they could kill him.

28:47 even though many false and bribed witnesses appeared, they could not find any false testimony.

28:48 At last, two witnesses stepped up and said, "He has said that God is not the Creator, but a man like you and me.

28:49 "He also said that he was begotten by a guardian angel of God, by the name of Gabriel."

28:50 Caiaphas, the high priest, arose and said to Jmmanuel, "Will you not reply to what these two are witnessing against you?"

28:51 But Jmmanuel kept quiet and smiled softly, and so the high priest said to him, "I swear by the living God that you told us you were begotten by the angel Gabriel, who is an angel of God, as foretold by the scriptures."

28:52 Jmmanuel spoke to him, "You say so. But I also tell you that god is not Creation, but he is the lord over the three human races that were begotten on earth through his will.

28:53 "God has come from the far distances of the universe and brought the world under his will, so he is the supreme emperor of these three human races,

28:54 "one of which is here in this country, which you have deprived of its rights and subjugated, another in the East as far as the land of India, and the third in the North from the land of the king with horns to the sea where icy mountains drift in the water.

28:55 "There are seven human races living in all the directions of the wind, from one end of the earth to the other.

28:56 "God is also lord over them, even though they serve other gods who are also not of this earth.

28:57 "If you consider god as Creation, you are mistaken, and violating the truth.

28:58 "Just as you and I are human, so god is human too, except he is spiritually and in his consciousness more advanced than the human races created by him.

28:59 "God and his celestial sons are other human races that have come from the far distances of the universe in their machines made of metal.

28:60 "Creation alone stands immeasurably higher than god and his celestial sons, who are the guardian angels.

28:61 "Alone Creation is the incalculable secret that begets life and thus stands immeasurably higher above god and all life.

28:62 "Understand the truth of this teaching, so that you may attain knowledge and wisdom in truth."

28:63 Then Caiaphas, the high priest, tore his clothes and spoke furiously, "He blasphemed God, the Creator. Why should we need further testimony against him? Behold, now you yourselves have heard his blasphemy.

28:64a "What punishment do you think he deserves?"

28:64b They answered, "He deserves death."

28:65 They beat him with their fists and spat into his face.

28:66 Some of them hit him from the back and said, "Prophesy, you great king of wisdom and son of a celestial son, who is it that is beating you?"

28:67 Peter had followed Jmmanuel and the group, and hid among the people who looked through the doors and windows. Thus he saw what was done to Jmmanuel.

28:68 Then a maid came up to him and said, "Aren't you one of the disciples of this Jmmanuel from Galilee?"

Chapter 29

The Denial of Peter

29:1 When Peter was asked by the maid, he denied it and said, "What kind of nonsense do you accuse me of? I don't know what you are saying."

29:2 But because of the maid's question, he was fearful and wanted to escape from there, because he was afraid for his life.

29:3 When he went out the door, another woman saw him and said to the people, "This man, too, was together with the blasphemer from Nazareth."

29:4 But Peter lied a second time, raised his hand to swear and said, "Truly, I don't know this confused person!"

29:5 And when Peter left the house, those who had been standing there came up to him, saying, "Aren't you one of those who serve this Jmmanuel? You are giving yourself away through your speech."

29:6 Peter started to revile Jmmanuel, cursed himself and swore, "I don't know this crazy person nor his blasphemous teachings of god!"

29:7 Soon thereafter a rooster crowed three times and Peter thought of the words of Jmmanuel, and he hurriedly ran away and cried bitterly.

The Suicide of Juda Ihariath

29:8 Juda Ihariot, the betrayer of Jmmanuel, was among the councilors who wanted to kill Jmmanuel.

29:9 But when he saw what bad injustice and torture were done to Jmmanuel, and that his face was bleeding, he felt repentant, and great distress and misery were in him.

29:10 At odds with himself, he took his money bag, threw it in front of the chief priests and elders of the council and said,

29:11 "I did an evil thing to this person because I was thinking only of gold and silver and goods and wealth.

29:12 "I repent that I betrayed innocent blood, because his teaching does not seem evil to me."

29:13a But the chief priests and elders said, "How does that concern us?

29:13b "Behold, it is up to you what you want to do to live in peace with yourself."

29:14 And Juda Ihariot cried and fled, and soon he hanged himself from a tree branch behind the walls of the city in the field of the potter.

29:15 The chief priests took the pieces of silver and said, "It is useless to put them into the collection box, because it is blood money. What shall we do with it?"

29:16 Then one of the sons of the elders came and said, "I followed Juda Ihariot and he has hanged himself from a branch of a tree in the field of the potter."

29:17 Caiaphas, the high priest said, "Well then, give the blood money to the potter and buy his field with it for the burial of strangers."

29:18 At dawn the next day the business was completed, and Juda Ihariot, the traitor of Jmmanuel, was the first to be buried in the field.

29:19 But the chief priests and elders of the council spread the news among the people that Judas Iscariot, the disciple of Jmmanuel, had hanged himself as a traitor and was buried in the field of the potter.

29:20 The people believed this talk, and they said, "He betrayed his friend for pieces of silver, and it serves him right that he hanged himself.

29:21 "He committed a capital crime, and from now on the field of the potter shall be named the Field of Blood."

29:22 Jmmanuel was brought before Pilate, the governor, who asked him, "Are you Jmmanuel, whom they call the 'king of wisdom?'"

Before Pilate

29:23 He said, "You have said it. That is what I am called by the people."

29:24 And Pilate said, "Is it also said that you were begotten by the angel Gabriel, who is an angel of God?"

29:25 Jmmanuel said, "You have said it."

29:26 Pilate said, "Let us hear your wisdom, because your teaching is new to me."

29:27 Jmmanuel replied, "Behold, eons ago, I returned from the realm of a higher world in order to fulfill a difficult task; and now I was begotten by a celestial son to be a prophet in this life. It happened according to destiny and the desire of god, the ruler over the human races of earth that were created by him.

29:28 "In addition to my knowledge of this next life, through his kindness I learned great insight and the right knowledge, which was imparted to me during forty days and forty nights by his teachers.

29:29 "Furthermore, I traveled much to faraway places and lived for many years in India. There I was taught much knowledge and many secrets by the great gurus and wise men, who are called masters.

29:30 "When I have fulfilled my mission here, I will go back there with my brother Thomas, who is a faithful disciple of mine."

29:31 When they heard Jmmanuel's speech, the elders and chief priests became very agitated and shouted in front of Pilate, "Do you hear his blasphemy?"

29:32 Pilate asked, "Don't you hear how severely they accuse you? Don't you wish to justify yourself?"

29:33a Jmmanuel answered, "Behold, I will carry my burden as it is destined.

29:33b "But it is also a fact that many are against me and will testify falsely; I will not find justice in this process.

29:34 "Truly, I say to you: Many dogs kill a hare, no matter how many turns it makes.

29:35 "It is also customary among people that the most just person does not find justice, because it does not matter whether many or few testify against him, as long as they are highly regarded.

29:36 "Justice rules only in the laws of nature, because they are the laws of Creation.

29:37 "But among people there is little justice, and they determine justice according to their social status and their wealth.

29:38 "Therefore I ask you, how could I expect justice by this standard?"

29:39 Pilate said, "Judging by the way you speak, you are very wise and I see no guilt in you.

29:40 "I question the teaching you just uttered, but in this, too, I see no evil, because all people should be blessed according to their faith.

29:41 "But since you have nothing to say regarding your innocence that would counter the denunciation of the chief priests and the elders, I have no hope for you, because their will is my command, which I have to obey."

29:42 Jmmanuel didn't answer him, which surprised the governor very much.

29:43 At the time of the Passover feast, governor Pilate was accustomed to releasing to the people whichever one of the prisoners they wanted, except those guilty of murder or causing death.

29:44 At this time he had a special prisoner named Barabbas.

29:45 When the people were gathered, Pilate asked them, "Which one do you want me to release, Barabbas, the criminal, or Jmmanuel, who is said to be a king of wisdom and the son of an angel?"

29:46 But he knew that the chief priests and elders had bribed the people by giving them copper, gold and silver for them to ask for the release of Barabbas and the death of Jmmanuel.

29:47 He knew very well that they had turned him over because of envy and hatred, since his teaching appealed to the people.

29:48 His wife also influenced Pilate by saying, "Don't have any dealings with this just man, because today I suffered greatly in my dreams on account of him, and I find his teaching to be good." Therefore, he was favorably inclined toward Jmmanuel.

29:49 But among the people there was much screaming and he asked again, "Which one shall I release?"

29:50 Slowly the screaming stopped, and the governor asked a third time, "Which one of these two shall I release?"

29:51 The people screamed, "Release Barabbas!"

29:52 And Pilate asked them, "Thus it shall be, but what shall I do with him who is said to be Jmmanuel, a king of wisdom?"

29:53 The people shouted, "Crucify him! Have him crucified!"

29:54a But the governor was not willing and asked very angrily, "What evil thing has he done that you want him crucified?

29:54b "He only taught a new doctrine, and for this he shall suffer death? Where then is the freedom of speech, thought and opinion?"

29:55 However, the people screamed even louder, "Have him crucified! Have him crucified!"

29:56 When Pilate realized there was great unrest and turmoil and that nothing could be done against these people who had been bribed, he took a pitcher of water and washed his hands before the people, saying,

29:57a "You know what you want to happen to him.

29:57b "He is the captive of the elders and chief priests, so let them judge him.

29:57c "I have nothing to do with this just man. I am not responsible for him, and I wash my hands before you in innocence."

29:58 But the people milled about, shouting, "He shall be crucified! He shall be crucified!"

29:59 Then Pilate turned Jmmanuel over to the chief priests and elders and released Barabbas to the people.

29:60 And the chief priests and elders had Jmmanuel whipped and handed him over to be crucified.

29:61 The people screamed and shouted and cursed Jmmanuel.

29:62 But the chief priests and elders indulged themselves in self-praise and were in good spirits because of the intrigue they had perpetrated.

Chapter 30

30:1 The soldiers of the governor agreed with the chief priests and the elders and, dragging Jmmanuel with them into the court house, they brought the entire crowd with them.

30:2 They undressed him and put a purple coat on him,

30:3 made a wreath of thorns, placed it on his head, put a cane into his right hand, bent their knees before him and said,

30:4 "We greet you, great king of wisdom of the Judeans."

30:5 And they spat on him, took the cane out of his hand, and beat him with it on the head until blood ran over his face.

30:6 When he was miserable and bleeding, Caiaphas, the high priest, asked, "What are you going to do now, great king of wisdom?"

30:7 But Jmmanuel was quiet, saying not a word.

30:8 They hit him again on the head, and he sighed in pain and started to speak: "As it is written in the old prophets, that I am the king of wisdom of the Judeans, it hits the truth; so I am the true prophet of all human races on earth; but in all truth I am not the prophet of those confused Israelites who call themselves sons and daughters of Zion.

30:9 "Truly, I say to you, if you beat and mock me, you shall be beaten and mocked by those whom you, since ancient times, have enslaved and whose land you and your forefathers have plundered.

30:10 "And the time will come in five times 100 years when you will have to atone for this, when the legitimate owners of the land enslaved by you will begin to rise against you and fight against you into the distant future.

30:11 "A new man will rise up in this land as a prophet and will rightfully condemn and persecute you and you will have to pay with your blood.

30:12 "This man will create a forceful new sect especially for preserving the truthful teaching and will have himself recognized as a prophet and in so doing persecute you through all times.

30:13 "Even though, according to your claim, he will be a false prophet and you will revile him, he will nevertheless be a true prophet, and he will have great power, and he will have your race persecuted throughout all time in the future.

30:14 "His name will be Mohammed, and his name will bring horror, misery and death to your kind, which you deserve.

30:15 "Truly, truly, I say to you: His name will be written for you with blood, and his hatred against your kind will be endless.

30:16 "Since he will be a true prophet, but according to you a false one, he will bring you a doctrine that will seem to you confusing and unintelligible, and his rising sect will eventually be finished when his and your followers will lay the foundation for a bloody end, because his teaching will be distorted and falsified and end in an evil and wrong sect."

30:17 And as he talked that way, the chief priests and members of the council of elders seethed in rage and beat him so hard that he collapsed and whimpered.

30:18 After they had beaten and mocked him, they took off his coat, put only his garments back on and led him away to crucify him.

30:19 They placed upon his right shoulder a heavy wooden cross, so that he himself would carry this great burden to the place of his death.

30:20 But the cross was heavy, and Jmmanuel moaned under this burden, and his blood combined with his sweat into a vile mixture.

30:21 Jmmanuel collapsed under the heavy burden, because his strength left him.

30:22 But when a stranger came along named Simon of Cyrene, they forced him to help carry the cross.

30:23 Soon they came to the place called Golgotha.

30:24 His path there was difficult, because he was reviled, beaten and mocked.

30:25 They gave him wine to drink mixed with urine taken from animals.

30:26 When he tasted it, he did not want to drink it, so they beat him to make him drink.

30:27 Then they forced him down on the cross, beating him. They nailed his hands and feet onto the wood. They did it this way for the first time, contrary to custom, because until then the crucified were tied to the cross.

30:28 After they had nailed him on and put the cross upright, they shared his clothing among themselves by casting a lot.

30:29 They sat there and watched him so that no one would come and take him off the cross.

30:30 Two murderers were crucified with him, one to his right and one to his left, with him in the middle.

30:31 Those who were around him blasphemed, mocked and ridiculed him.

30:32 They shouted, "Since you are the king of wisdom, help yourself!

30:33 "Since you are the son of a celestial son and possess great power, why don't you get off the cross?"

30:34 The scribes, Pharisees, chief priests and elders of the people likewise mocked him, saying,

30:35a "You helped others, but you cannot help yourself.

30:35b "Since you are a king of wisdom, get down from the cross and help yourself.

30:35c "If you do that, we will believe in you and your teaching.

30:36a "He trusted in his wisdom and in being the son of the angel Gabriel.

30:36b "Thus, may his wisdom or the angel Gabriel save him now if he so fancies."

30:37 Likewise, the murderers crucified to his right and left mocked and reviled him.

30:38 Then the sky clouded over, the sun became dark, and a great storm arose across the land, which happened not often at that time of year, but only occasionally.

30:39 The terrible storm roared for three hours before the sun broke through the clouds again.

30:40 At that time Jmmanuel cried out, “I’m thirsty! Give me something to drink.”

30:41 Then one of the chief priests got a sponge, soaked it in vinegar, put it on a pole and gave it to him to drink.

30:42 When the others saw that, they scolded the man, saying, “Stop! Do not give him any more to drink. Let us see how long he can bear this.”

30:43 Behold, a last great thunder clap ended the storm, the whole land trembled, and the earth shook.

30:44 With the tremendous thunder clap all about, Jmmanuel cried out again, but nobody understood him, because his speech was confused.

30:45 Then his head fell forward, he slipped into near-death, and they thought he was dead.

30:46 A soldier took his lance and stabbed Jmmanuel in his loin to ensure that he was dead.

30:47 Blood mixed with water came from the wound, as is the case when a person is dead or near-dead.

30:48 Since the soldier thought that Jmmanuel was dead, he informed the others.

30:49 They were all astonished, because it was unusual for those crucified to die so quickly.

30:50 But since the soldier told them, they believed him and went away.

30:51 Among them were also many women and others who watched from the distance, because they were followers of Jmmanuel and had served him and followed him from Galilee.

30:52 Among them were Mary, the mother of Jmmanuel, Mary Magdalene and others.

30:53 After the soldiers had left, they went to him, knelt before the cross and cried bitterly, because they, too, thought Jmmanuel was dead.

30:54 Also among them was Joseph of Arimathea, a follower of Jmmanuel.

30:55 After a little while, he noticed that Jmmanuel was only half dead, but he told no one.

Entombment

30:56 He quickly went into the city to see Pilate, and he asked for the body of Jmmanuel so that he could bury him.

30:57 Pilate ordered that Jmmanuel be turned over to Joseph.

30:58 Many people went with him and they took Jmmanuel off the cross. Joseph wrapped the body in pure linen that he had previously painted so as to form an image of Jmmanuel.

30:59 Joseph of Arimathea carried the body of Jmmanuel all the way to Jerusalem and placed him outside the city in his own tomb, which he had cut into a rock for his own future burial.

30:60 He rolled a big stone in front of the door of the tomb and went to obtain some medicine in order to nurse Jmmanuel.

30:61 The entrance of the tomb was guarded by soldiers and Jmmanuel's mother so no one could enter and steal the body.

30:62 Joseph of Arimathea sought out Jmmanuel's friends from India and went back with them to the tomb. They went in through a secret second entrance unknown to the henchmen and to the soldiers and nursed him for three days and three nights, so that he was soon in better health again and his strength was restored.

30:63 The tomb was guarded on the other side by the soldiers, because the chief priests and Pharisees had gone to Pilate, saying,

30:64 "Governor, we considered that when this crazy man was still alive, he said to the people, 'I shall return after three days and three nights and rise, because I will be only half dead.'

30:65 "But, since it was established through a soldier that he was really dead, his tomb should be guarded so that no one can come, steal the body and say, 'Behold, he has risen from the dead after all!'

30:66 "Therefore, command that the tomb be guarded for three days so that the last deception may not be worse than the first."

30:67 Pilate said, "Take my soldiers as guardians. Go and watch the tomb as well as possible."

30:68 They went away, watched the tomb, and sealed the stone in front of the door.

30:69 But they did not know the secret of the grave, namely, that it had two exits and entrances, so that Jmmanuel's helpers could, without being seen, go to him to apply healing salves and herbs, so that on the third day he was again strong enough to walk.

Chapter 31

Jmmanuel's Flight from the Tomb

31:1 When the first day of the week had come after Passover, the three days and nights had passed following which Jmmanuel would live again after near-death, as he had foretold.

31:2 Behold, a great thunder arose in the air, and a radiant light came down from the sky and landed on the earth, not far from the tomb.

31:3 Then a guardian angel came out of the light, and his appearance was like lightning and his garment was as white as snow.

31:4 He went to the tomb, and the soldiers got out of his way because they feared him.

31:5 He lifted his hand from which came bright lightning that hit the soldiers one after the other.

31:6 And they fell to the ground and did not stir for a long time.

31:7 Then the guardian angel stepped up to the tomb, rolled the stone away from the door and said to Mary, the mother of Jmmanuel, and to Mary Magdalene, who were both there,

31:8 "Do not be afraid. I know that you are seeking Jmmanuel, the crucified.

31:9 "But he is not here. He lives, as he said. Come here and behold the place where he lay.

31:10 "Go quickly and tell his disciples that he has risen from near-death.

31:11 "Also tell them he will walk ahead of you to Galilee, and there you will see him. Behold, I have told you."

31:12 But Mary asked, "Yet he was dead and lay here dead, how can he rise?"

31:13 The guardian angel answered, "Why are you seeking someone alive among the dead?

31:14 "Go now and spread the news among his disciples, but beware, and do not tell anyone else."

31:15 The guardian angel went to the bright light and disappeared into it; soon a great thunder came out of it again, and it rose up into the air, shooting straight into the sky.

31:16 Jmmanuel's mother and Mary Magdalene went away, leaving the tomb.

31:17 The soldiers recovered from their paralysis and were surprised; so they went into the city and spread the news of what had happened.

31:18 And they came together with the chief priests and elders of the council for a secret meeting to decide what to tell the people.

31:19 The chief priests and elders gave a lot of money to the soldiers and said, "Tell the people his disciples came at night while we were sleeping and stole his body."

31:20 And the soldiers took the money and did as they had been instructed.

31:21 Mary and Mary Magdalene went away and did as they had been told by the guardian angel.

31:22 Behold, a guardian angel met them again on their way and said, "Remember what you have been told. Be careful not to make a mistake when talking to the people."

31:23 Mary Magdalene approached the guardian angel, who wore a brilliant white garment, and she wanted to grasp his hand.

31:24 But he stepped back from her and said, "Don't touch me, because I am of a kind different than you and my garment is a protection against this world.

31:25 "If you touch me, you will die and be consumed by fire.

31:26 "Get away from me, and do as you have been told."

31:27 So they went away, met Peter and another disciple and told them what had happened.

31:28 Peter and the other disciple went to the tomb, the other disciple arriving there first.

31:29 He looked into the tomb and saw the linen shrouds lying neatly on the ground, but he did not enter.

31:30a Peter also came, went into the tomb and found everything just as the other disciple had.

31:30b The shrouds had been carefully folded and placed on the ground, and the sweat cloth that had been on Jmmanuel's head had been placed on a particular spot, together with the salves and herbs and peculiar figures of clay such as he had never seen before, and so they were strange to him.

Jmmanuel Meets with His Disciples

31:32 In the evening of the same day, the disciples were gathered in a room in the city where they had taken their last meal with Jmmanuel before Passover.

31:33 They were speaking to each other about what had happened during the day, behold, the door opened and a stranger whom they had never seen before entered.

31:34 And they were afraid that he might be one of the Israelites wanting to betray them.

31:35 But then the stranger said, "Peace be with you," and when he took the cloth from his face, they recognized him as Jmmanuel.

31:36 When he had said that, he showed them his hands, loin and feet. They saw his wounds and were happy that he was among them.

31:37 But Thomas believed a ghost to be in front of him. So he said, "If I could touch your wounds, I would know that you are not a ghost."

31:38 Jmmanuel said to him, "Reach out and place your hand on my wounds, so that you of little faith may recognize the truth."

31:39 So Thomas did as he had been told, and he touched his wounds and said, "Truly, it is you."

31:40 Then Jmmanuel went away, saying, "Keep the secret of my return, so it will not become known that I am alive."

31:41 Behold, the next day the disciples set out for Galilee to spread the joyful news among the followers of Jmmanuel.

31:42 As other followers went along the way, behold, an itinerant joined them and walked with them part of the way.

31:43 They were sad and talked among themselves about how Jmmanuel had been forced to die on the cross.

31:44 Then the itinerant, a stranger, said to them, "Why are you mourning?" And they told him what grieved them.

31:45 But he said to them, "You of such little faith, Jmmanuel told you he would rise from near-death after three days and nights,

31:46 "and so it happened as he said."

31:47 After he had spoken he took the cloth from his face and they recognized him as Jmmanuel.

31:48 But he said nothing more, covered his face again and went away. And he was not seen for a long time.

31:49 Long after Jmmanuel had disappeared, it happened that the disciples were fishing on the Sea of Tiberias,

31:50 and they caught nothing the whole night, so by daybreak they were exasperated.

31:51 When they came to the shore, there stood a stranger who asked, "Haven't you anything to eat? I am hungry."

31:52 They answered, "No, we have not caught one fish in our nets."

31:53 Then the stranger said, "Throw the net out to the right side of the boat, and you will bring in a large haul."

31:54 The disciples were astonished by what he said and threw out the net. And behold, they could not pull it in because of the multitude of fish.

31:55 They came ashore and prepared a meal, because, like the stranger, they were hungry.

31:56 He uncovered his face, and, behold, it was Jmmanuel.

31:57 And while they were eating and in good spirits, he said to them, "Go to Galilee to such and such mountain; there I will join you, because our time together has ended and each one may go his own way."

Chapter 32

Jmmanuel's Farewell

32:1 They went to the mountain to which Jmmanuel had directed them.

32:2 they had gathered there, he said to them, "Behold, I will talk to you one last time; then I will leave and never return.

32:3 "My path leads me to India where many of this human race also dwell, because they left this land to live there.

32:4 "My mission leads me to them and to the human race that was born there.

32:5 "My path there will be long, because I have yet to bring my old teaching, newly presented, to many countries, likewise to the shores of the great black waters to the north of here.

32:6 "Before I leave you, I will give you my last instruction of the teaching, as follows:

32:7 "If people live according to the laws of Creation, they live correctly in truth, but here is the final goal:

32:8 "Everything human in people has to die, but everything creative in them has to rise and embrace Creation.

32:9 "Consider the universe as the place where Creation lives in infinity.

32:10 "Everything that people possess has its origin in Creation; therefore it belongs to Creation.

32:11 "People shall change their entire spiritual lives and perfect them, so that they will become one with Creation.

32:12 "Whatever people do, they shall do it with the awareness of the presence of Creation.

32:13 "But they shall never try to force truth onto another, because it would be only half its worth.

32:14 "First, people shall watch their own progress in consciousness and spirit so as to produce creative harmony within themselves.

32:15 "No greater darkness rules in people than ignorance and lack of wisdom.

32:16 "The victory of humanity in its greatness consists of destroying and removing each power opposing the creative spirit, so that the creative spirit may win.

32:17 "People should develop their power to judge good and evil and to understand correctly all things, so that they may be wise and fair and follow the laws.

32:18 "It is necessary to understand what is real and unreal, what is valuable and not valuable, what is of Creation and not of Creation.

32:19 "People have to become a universal oneness, so that they become one with Creation.

32:20 "Make your lives equal to the laws of nature, then you will live according to the laws of Creation.

32:21 "No matter how great the suffering of people, the power of Creation in them to conquer all that is evil is immeasurably greater.

32:22 "If people live only in their consciousness as humans, they are inaccessibly far from their spirits, from Creation and hence its laws.

32:23 "The greater people's dedication is to the laws of Creation, the deeper shall be the peace within themselves.

32:24 "People's happiness consists in seeking and finding the truth, so that they may gather knowledge and wisdom and think and act in accord with Creation.

32:25 "Only through the conditions of human life can they develop and use their creative powers in consciousness and spirit.

32:26 "People obtain experience in the use of their powers and capabilities only by trying daily to unfold them.

32:27-28 "So long as people do not become one with Creation, they will never be able to rise above death or near-death, since fear of the unknown is in them; and only when they can fully recognize the perfection and unity of Creation can they slowly gain eminence.

32:29 "Instead of being guided by instincts and impulses, people should live according to knowledge and wisdom so that they may live justly according to the laws and commandments.

32:30 "People shall not lose their way in the forest of limitations, but shall expand their consciousness and seek and find knowledge, logic and truth, and from it learn wisdom,

32:31 "so that they may come closer to their lives' goal and recognize the creative principle in all things.

32:32 Thousands of lights will guide them on their paths, if they watch and follow them.

32:33 "People will attain all their knowledge and wisdom, if they seriously strive for perfection.

32:34 "The laws serve all those who are willing to seek truth in unlimited measure and to learn wisdom from it,

32:35 "inasmuch as they master within themselves all possible dimensions, develop their spiritual powers higher and higher and in so doing perfect themselves.

32:36 "People should try not to dwell upon their physical misery, but upon the reality of the spirit and the existence of Creation.

32:37 "There is a constant restlessness in people, because they have a premonition that Creation is their fate and destination.

32:38 "They may be great, wise and good, yet that is not sufficient, because they can always become greater, wiser and better;

32:39 "there may not be any limits to love, peace and joy, because the present has to be constantly exceeded.

32:40 "Truly, I say to you: A love that is unlimited, lasting and infallible is without conditions and pure and will burn in its fire all that is unclean and evil,

32:41 "for such a love is the love of Creation and hence its laws, for which humanity has been predestined since the beginning of time.

32:42 "Since this is the final goal of humanity, people must take care that this must and shall be so, for this is their destiny.

32:43 "But as yet people do not understand the wisdom of this teaching, so it is being adulterated everywhere on earth.

32:44 "In their ignorance people falsify it in various ways and forms so that it becomes diffused and unintelligible.

32:45 "But in two thousand years it will be taught anew and unfalsified, when people have become reasonable and knowledgeable, and a new age foretells great upheavals.

32:46-7 "It can be read in the stars that the people of the new era will be great revolutionaries. Therefore, a few special selected people, the new proclaimers of my teaching, will preach it unfalsified and with great courage.

32:48 "But you, go and prepare the way for my teaching and make all peoples its disciples.

32:49 "However, beware of false teachings, which you might allow to arise because of your ignorance, since some of you are inclined that way.

32:50 "Teach them to follow everything that I have commanded you, so that you do not falsify my teaching."

32:51 After he talked to them that way, a thundering came from the sky, and a great light descended.

32:52 The light landed on the ground not far from them, and it had a metallic glitter in the sunshine.

32:53 Jmmanuel no longer spoke, but went away to the metallic light and entered into it.

32:54 Then a haze arose all around it. Once again, a thundering occurred and the light ascended back into the sky.

32:55 And the disciples secretly returned to Jerusalem and announced to like-minded people what had happened.

Chapter 33

33:1 Jmmanuel was let off by the great light in Syria and lived in Damascus for two years without being recognized.

33:2 After this time, he sent a messenger to Galilee to look for his brother Thomas and his disciple Judas Iscariot.

33:3 months passed before they joined Jmmanuel and brought bad news.

33:4 Thomas said, "Your disciples greatly falsified your teachings, insulting you as the son of god and at the same time making you equal to Creation.

33:5 "The chief priests and elders persecute your followers and stone them when they can catch them.

33:6 "Thomas, one of your disciples, fled, and it is reported that he left for the land of India with a caravan.

33:7 "A great enemy of yours has arisen in a man named Saul.

33:8 "He is fuming with rage and utters death threats against your disciples and those who trust in your teaching.

33:9 "He is having letters written to the synagogues in all countries in order to find those who follow your new teaching, bind them and take them to Jerusalem.

33:10 "No distinction is to be made among women, men and children, because they will all be found guilty and put to death."

33:11 But Jmmanuel said, "Don't be afraid, the time will soon come when Saul will be apprised of his evil thinking.

33:12 "He is already on his way here, following you and Judas Iscariot to Damascus, in order to seize you both and take you to Jerusalem in shackles.

33:13 "But I will confront him before he reaches Damascus; since he believes me to be dead, he will presume he is seeing a ghost."

33:14 Jmmanuel set out to see a friend who was helpful to him with secret things involving powders, salves and liquids that smelled bad.

33:15 Well supplied with these things he departed and left the city along the road to Galilee.

33:16 A day's trip from Damascus, he waited in the rocks and prepared his concoction.

33:17 During the night he saw a group of men coming, among them Saul, the persecutor of his disciples.

33:18 When they were close, he struck a fire and threw it into his concoction, which produced a tremendously bright light that blinded the group.

33:19 Jmmanuel continued poking the flaring concoction, so that huge lightnings, stars and fireballs shot into the sky or fell down from it, accompanied by thundering booms and strong hissing sounds, as if coming from gigantic dragons and serpents.

33:20 The thunder bolts and booms subsided and so did the hissing; and the blinding lightnings and the multi-colored fires died down, yet stinging smoke still covered the land and caused the group to cough and shed tears.

33:21 Then Jmmanuel called out, "Saul, Saul, why do you persecute my disciples?"

33:22 Saul, however, was afraid and fell onto the ground, crying out, "Who are you who speaks to me like this?"

33:23 Jmmanuel answered, "I am Jmmanuel whom you persecute in your hatred, along with my disciples.

33:24 "Get up. Go into the city and let yourself be taught how you should live."

33:25 Saul was very much afraid and said, "But you are the one who was crucified. So you are dead and speak to me as a ghost."

33:26 Jmmanuel did not answer him. He went away and headed for Damascus.

33:27 But the men who were Saul's companions stood still, frozen with fear, because they also thought they had heard a ghost.

33:26 Saul got up from the ground and opened his eyes. However, he saw nothing because his eyes were blinded by the bright light that Jmmanuel had caused.

33:27 His companions took him by the hand and led him to Damascus,

33:28 and for three days he did not see, eat or drink anything.

33:29 A disciple of Jmmanuel came to Saul and preached to him the new teaching, so that he slowly understood it.

33:30 But because of the events near the rocks, he was slightly dazed in his consciousness, so that he misunderstood much and talked in a confused manner.

33:31 Somewhat bewildered in his consciousness, he went away and preached incoherently to the people.

33:32 Jmmanuel stayed another thirty days in Damascus and leaked the news that he would presently leave the country and travel to the land of India.

33:33 His mother Mary came from Nazareth and set out on the road to the land of India with Jmmanuel, his brother Thomas and Judas Iscariot.

33:34 And Jmmanuel started to preach again, teaching the people wherever he found them along the way and in any settlement he came to.

33:35 The strength in him was new and his teaching more powerful than before.

Chapter 34

The Teaching of the Creation

34:1 Jmmanuel preached powerfully saying, "Behold, Creation is above humanity, above god and above everything.

34:2 "Creation seems perfect to people's comprehension, but that is not so.

34:3 "Since Creation is spirit and thus lives, it also has to perfect itself forever.

34:4 "But since Creation is one within itself, it can perfect itself only through the creation and generation of new spirit, which lives in people and invigorates them and becomes progressive through its learning and perfects itself.

34:5 "The newly generated spirit is part of Creation itself, but it is still ignorant in every detail.

34:6 "When a new spirit has been created, which is still ignorant in every way, it lives in a person's body and begins to learn.

34:7 "People think the ignorant spirit is stupid, and they say that such persons are confused.

34:8 "But they are not, because they are only ignorant and devoid of knowledge and wisdom.

34:9 "So let this new spirit live a life within the person to gather knowledge.

34:10 "When this spirit goes into the beyond, it is no longer as ignorant as at its beginning.

34:11 "It comes back into the world and lives as a human being, but no longer quite as ignorant as at its inception.

34:12 "Again it learns and gathers further knowledge and new wisdom, so it escapes from ignorance more and more.

34:13 "The time comes after many renewed lives that people view this spirit as normal and not confused.

34:14 "But this is neither the end of the spirit nor fulfillment, because, having become knowing, the spirit now seeks the greatest wisdom,

34:15 "so that the human being may perfect itself to the point of unfolding its creativity, finally becoming one with Creation, as was its destiny from the beginning.

34:16-17 "Thus Creation has brought forth a new spirit, allowing it to be perfected independently in the human body, and the perfected spirit returns to Creation to become one with it; in this way Creation perfects itself, because within it is the knowledge and wisdom that enables it to do so.

34:18 "Truly, I say to you: The time will never come when Creation stops creating new spirits and broadening itself.

34:19 "Creation also needs rest, and when it is not creating, it sleeps, as is proper for all living things.

34:20 "As human life is divided into day and night and work and rest, so Creation also has its times of work and rest.

34:21 "Its period, however, is different from that of people, because its laws are the laws of the spirit,

34:22 "but human laws are the laws of material life.

34:23 "Material life is limited, but the life of the spirit lasts forever and knows no end.

34:24 "Creation is subject to the laws of Original Duration and Original Creation, which is the absolute of absolutes and the beginning and endlessness of everything and created out of itself.

34:25 "Its secret is that which is immeasurable and is based on the number seven, which is counted in 'times.'

34:26 "This is one of the secrets and laws that the human mind will solve only in perfection.

34:27 "But be it said that the laws of life are not hidden from wise persons, hence they can recognize and follow them.

34:28-29 "If the wise understand that the secret of Original Creation lies everywhere in the calculations based upon the number seven, they will obtain and possess the knowledge that Creation has a time for work or rest that is also counted by the number seven.

34:30 "Creation rested in the lap of slumber for seven great times, so that nothing existed, not even the universe.

34:31 "Creation only slumbered and did not bring forth a creature or anything.

34:32 "However, it awakened from its slumber and began to create everything after sleeping through the seven periods of the seven great times.

34:33-34 "After having rested for seven periods and seven great times, it now creates everything for seven more periods and seven great times, until it requires rest again and lies down anew in deep slumber for seven great times.

34:35 "Since it will rest again and lie down to sleep, nothing will exist except Creation itself.

34:36 "There will be no more creatures or any other thing.

34:37 "Only Creation will exist in the seven periods and seven great times, because it will rest and slumber until it awakes again and brings forth new creatures and everything else.

34:38 "Since Creation is one in itself, all life, enduring and existent, will be one in itself.

34:39 "It is the law of Creation that proves that all humans, plants and animals and all life are one in themselves.

34:40 "If a person believes everything is two or three, he is wrong, because everything is one.

34:41 "Whatever a person believes to be two or three is actually one, so he should make everything that is two or three into one.

34:42 "Since the spirit in a person is part of Creation, it is one with Creation; consequently it is not two.

34:43 "Since the body is a part of the spirit in a different form and matter, it is therefore one with the spirit; consequently it is not two.

34:44 "The teaching is that somehow there is unity, not duality or trinity in any other form.

34:45 “If it appears to people that there is a duality or trinity, they are the victims of deception, because they do not think logically but according to human knowledge.

34:46 “But if they think according to the knowledge of the spirit, they find the logic, which is also in the law.

34:47 “Only human thinking can be incorrect, not the laws of Creation.

34:48 “That is why it is said that everything emanates from a unity, and duality is apparent only because people cannot grasp the truth in their limited thinking.

34:49 “Since everything is unity and everything emanates from it, no duality or trinity whatsoever can exist because it would violate the laws of Creation.

34:50 “Therefore people should make the two into one and think and act according to the laws of Creation.

34:51 “Only in his ignorance does man fabricate duality and violate the laws of Creation.

34:52 “When he aligns everything with unity, making all into one, and then says to a mountain: ‘Move away,’ it will move away.

34:53 “Since everything is one in Creation, in its laws, in the creatures and in matter, it is without error.

34:54 “When a wise man says that there are always two of everything, he means that they are one within themselves and one together.

34:55 “It is only two in appearance, because in itself and also together it is always one.

34:56 “Therefore evil is one in itself because it is also good in itself. Likewise, good is one in itself because it is just as much evil in itself.

34:57 “Since they are one and unity apart, they are also one and unity together, because that is the law of Creation.

34:58 “Thus the result is that there are two parts in appearance, but they are both one in themselves and one when together.

34:59 “If people say that a trinity also exists, their consciousness is confused by some kinds of sects, wrong teachings or falsified thinking.

34:60 "A unit always consists of two parts that are one in themselves, but are two only in appearance.

34:61 Since a person is a unit of two parts, the spirit is a unit in two parts, but both one in themselves and one together.

34:62 "The body cannot live without the spirit, and conversely, because spirit and body are a unit despite their seeming duality.

34:63 "The spirit lives according to the same law, because in itself it consists of two parts and is one in each part; thus it is one in itself.

34:64 "The two parts of the spirit are wisdom and strength.

34:65 "Without wisdom, the power of the spirit cannot be utilized, nor can any wisdom emerge without spiritual power.

34:66 "Thus there are always two things needed which are one in themselves, so there is a oneness in the unity but not a duality.

34:67 "The law says that persons are unities within themselves consisting of two equal parts that are a unity both in themselves and together.

34:68 "However, body and spirit, each of which constitutes a unit in itself, are the two equal parts in people.

34:69 "When the scribes teach that a person lives in a trinity, this teaching is erroneous and falsified, because it is not taught according to the laws of Creation."

Chapter 35

Cults About Jmmanuel

35:1 It came to pass that Jmmanuel, his mother Mary and his brother Thomas traveled along to the cities near the sea in the North. Since time immemorial, warlike women lived there whose descendants, however, were now peace-loving.

35:2 He preached the new teaching to them according to his knowledge but had to flee from their cities because they tried to kill him.

35:3 Their own teaching, far removed from truth, was from a strict sect, and they punished with death followers of other teachings.

35:4 These people outlawed Jmmanuel and persecuted him as a rebel against their sect, so he fled.

35:5 It came to pass during his flight that he met a large caravan. He and his following joined it and went inland and into the mountains.

35:6 They traveled through the central part of the country for many weeks and came to another sea and into the city of Ephesus.

35:7-8 But Jmmanuel was very much afraid and no longer preached his new teaching so that no one would recognize him, because in Ephesus there were many people, dealers and merchants, who came there from Jerusalem to conduct business.

35:9 There were many among them who knew Jmmanuel but felt hostile toward him; therefore he left them and veiled his face.

35:10 The dealers and merchants in Ephesus had spread the story of Jmmanuel and his supposed death, which had occurred two and a half years earlier.

35:11 However, after he had stayed in the city for a few days, behold, one of the merchants recognized him and informed those of like mind who belonged to a secret group called the Association of the Essenes.

35:12 They took Jmmanuel to a meeting that was secret because their association was not permitted and they feared the people.

35:13 Among them was one named Juthan, the oldest of the secret association in Jerusalem, who said,

35:14 "Behold, we know very well what happened to you in your life, but we do not know why you are still among the living. So, do tell us your secret."

35:15 But Jmmanuel was afraid that he would be tied up and returned to Jerusalem if he reported everything to the Association of the Essenes.

35:16 Yet he told them what had happened and how he fled from Jerusalem and came there.

35:17 Juthan, the eldest, said, "Behold, we belong to a secret group called the Association of the Essenes.

35:18 "Our seeking and knowledge are not attuned to the teachings of the scribes, but to the secrets of nature and everything that is inexplicable to people.

35:19 "You are great in your knowledge, and by all measure you have progressed in knowledge far beyond us and the Pharisees, the astrologers, and even the elders and wise men.

35:20 "Therefore, join our group, be one of us and teach us your knowledge."

35:21 But Jmmanuel answered, "Even if I should teach you my knowledge, it would not agree with your teachings because you follow human wisdom, whereas I adhere to spiritual wisdom.

35:22 "Therefore I think that our different teachings will be incompatible with one another.

35:23 "It is not my inclination to spread my knowledge and teaching secretly, as you do, because your secret association is not permitted.

35:24 "But let me think over the pros and cons for three days, because I must think about everything before I give you my last word on it. Then I will tell you yes or no."

35:25a Juthan said, "Be it as you say.

35:25b "Peace be with you.

35:25c "Go, and give us your answer in three days, if you want to."

35:26 But Jmmanuel went away, fleeing from the city with his following, and traveled east, far into the country.

35:27 Jmmanuel said to his followers, "Behold, the Essenes live in a false sect, though their followers gather much of my teaching.

35:28 "Their old doctrine, however, is not the teaching of truth, knowledge, love, logic, wisdom and laws of Creation; therefore it is false and worthless.

35:29 "They have recognized this and are now weaving my doctrine of truth into their teaching of half-truths, to create a new sect, and they demean me by calling me one of them.

35:30 "They will claim that I am connected with their association and that they had helped me from the beginning of my life.

35:31 "They will also say that my teaching stemmed from the knowledge of their sect and that they had saved me from the cross as one of them.

35:32 "They will also claim that all my followers were from their sect

35:33 "and that I am the Son of God.

35:34 "But I tell you that I never belonged to this association of Essenes, and that I have nothing in common with it or its followers, and I never received any help from them.

35:35 "The Association of the Essenes is not the only group that will make use of my name. Many sects will come forth in my name and thereby consider themselves great and want to appear this way before all people.

35:36 "Thus, strange sects will arise and glorify me to make themselves more credible, so as to enslave more people.

35:37 "Many sects will be established in my name, but only for the purpose of enslaving the human consciousness and freedom, thereby bringing great power over the people and their land and money.

35:38 "But I tell you that no sect is just unless it recognizes Creation alone as the highest power and lives according to its laws and commandments.

35:39 "There will be no sect which preaches truth, knowledge and wisdom.

35:40 "It will be two times a thousand years before the time comes when my teaching will be preached anew, without being falsified, when the condition of false teachings and sects, the lies, cheating and deceit of the conjurers of the dead and spirits, the soothsayers and clairvoyants as well as the charlatans will be at their peak.

35:41 "Until then, there will be so many false sects, liars, impostors, charlatans, conjurers of the dead and spirits, false soothsayers, clairvoyants and false mediums who claim to be extraterrestrial, from other dimensions and coming from the distant depths of the universe, that they can no longer be counted.

35:42 "They will be built on human blood, hatred, greed and power, lies, deception, trickery, misunderstanding, self-deceit, confusion of consciousness and mania.

35:43 "But after they have been established they shall be destroyed, because the truth shall triumph,

35:44 "for there is no untruth that shall not be denounced as a lie.

35:45 "There is nothing hidden that shall not become evident.

35:46 "People shall recognize what is in front of their faces, and what is hidden from them will reveal itself, provided they search for truth and the explanation derived from wisdom.

35:47 "But the truth lies deep and within the laws of Creation, and mankind shall seek and find it there alone.

35:48 "Those who seek shall not stop seeking until they find,

35:49 "and when they find, they will be deeply shocked and astonished, but then they will rule over the universe.

35:50 "People shall recognize from this that the kingdom is within them and outside of them."

Chapter 36

Man and the Creation

36:1 It came to pass that Jmmanuel preached of humanity and Creation when he went east with a caravan.

36:2 He said, "Humanity shall look up to the stars, because majestic peace and grandeur rule there.

36:3 "There the infinite and timeless change takes place in unchangeable order through days and months and years, running into centuries, millennia and millions of years.

36:4 "Let humans also look down upon the earth, for there, too, is creative activity and timeless growth, being, passing, life and existence toward ever new developments.

36:5 "Greatness, dignity and beauty rule in harmony where nature is left to its own devices.

36:6 "But where traces of human order are active, pettiness, unruliness and ugliness testify to alarming disharmony.

36:7 "With inflated chest, man calls himself the crown of Creation, does not recognize Creation and sets people equal to it.

36:8 "But this man who tamed fire and rules the earth will not go very far.

36:9 "He will no doubt learn to control water and rule the earth, but in the process he will forget to recognize above him Creation and its laws.

36:10 "Thus, he will also forget to seek truth, knowledge, love, respect, life, logic, true freedom and wisdom,

36:11 "and will forget to live peacefully as man among men.

36:12 "His battle cry will be warfare, since he will want to attain power through violence.

36:13 "But when he thinks that he has the power in his hands, he uses it to enslave people, shed blood, exploit, commit brutality and crime, which ends in decline of morality.

36:14 "He will speak of honor, freedom and knowledge, but in reality it is nothing but hypocrisy, force and false teaching.

36:15 "Thus, in the future man will lose his face and display an evil and false mask.

36:16 "Many will degenerate into beasts and spend their earthly days in unconscious ignorance.

36:17 "Man's striving and thinking will be directed only toward acquisition, power, lust, mania and greed,

36:18 "and with his intellect he will arrange the things of this world to make them serve him, regardless of the fact that by so doing he destroys the laws of nature and nature itself in many ways.

36:19 "He will no longer believe in the timeless truths, which are anchored in the laws of nature.

36:20 "In his self-deception, he will find more meaning in human sciences than in all the values of the laws of nature and Creation.

36:21 "In their confusion, people will believe in this miserable philosophy of life they produced, which is caused by the false teachings of the sects and determinations of human laws and changes in the power structures in the various countries.

36:22 "People will want to control their lives by external means because they have forgotten how to become aware of their identities from the creative point of view.

36:23 "Thus they will delude, cheat and exploit their fellow men and the whole world with false means.

36:24-25 "And where there is some trust and truth left, they will change it into distrust and untruth, and in so doing they will get further and further away from the true life.

36:26 "Thus they will also lose sight of the principle of the oldest wisdom, which says that humans are the measure of all things in life, because they are after all a part of Creation.

36:27 "But the time will come for them when they must turn around and get back to the timeless values of life.

36:28 "In the beginning, only a few persons will know that people live not only on earth but also in the endless depths of the universe and that people live not only in the material world but that their spirits reach also into another world that cannot be perceived by the ordinary senses.

36:29-30 "The other finely woven world is the true home of the spirit, and therefore people should try without ceasing to attain a broadening and deepening of knowledge, love, truth, logic, true freedom, real peace, harmony and wisdom, so that the spirit may be perfected and lifted up into the true home, becoming one with Creation.

36:31 "Truly, I say to you: Those who understand the truth of this speech and attain understanding in wisdom are obliged to align their lives with their destiny of eternal change towards Creation.

36:32 "When people are honest and search, they will not know any preconceived opinion or prejudice.

36:33-34 "But the wise know and are aware of the law of the everlasting river of eternal change; therefore they endeavor to adjust to the great course of happenings, because they recognize the laws of Creation, that the cycles of life have to be closed through the determinations of the laws.

36:35 Wherever life reveals itself, it is based upon the law of the invisible secret that brings about the eternal change.

36:36 "Whoever disregards and fails to recognize timeless and imperishable laws and truths will have to suffer evil consequences.

36:37 "Lies and hatred will blind such a person and even entire peoples, and they will rush into the abyss of their own destruction.

36:38 "A blind, destructive mania will come over them, and the heroes among them will be the greatest destroyers.

36:39 "Discord will permeate people's entire lives, and there is no longer a unity or perfection when there is a split.

36:40 "As long as there is imperfection in life, people will have to bear these consequences: sickness, misery, injustice, need, fighting, strife, slavery, false sects and exploitation leading to bloodshed and death.

36:41 "So let the human beware and wake up, because the laws of Creation say that only that which is timeless and everlasting is of permanence, truth and wisdom, and so it is."

NOTES:

NOTES:

NOTES:

NOTES:

NOTES:

NOTES:

NOTES:

To order see page 189 for prices and bonus offer.

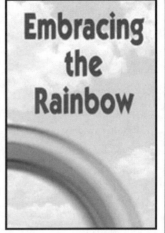

Becoming

The messages contained in this, the third book, are offered for the continued realization of who and what each human being truly is. The consciousness changing information each volume contains brings forth the understanding that humanity on this planet is, in reality, a whole and holy awareness. From the global myriad of belief systems arises a single picture that represents a composite awareness. This totality of thought creates the reality of the human experience. A great deal of effort is now focused with the intent of influencing how the individual and the total global awareness perceive the human experience. The mind discerns what it understands is its surrounding reality but the feelings determine its believability. Confusion masks the ability to choose between what appears to be true and what the feelings believe to be true. Beneath all the rhetoric that is focused on the conscious and subconscious levels within the current deluge of information in all its various forms is the human desire for the freedom to choose what is for the highest and best good of each individual and the planetary whole. Mankind stands at the threshold, the decision point of whether to accept what it is being told is for its highest and best good or to instead shrug off the programmed suggestions and choose for itself a future that is in total contrast. At the heart of the matter is the opportunity to choose cooperation rather than competition, brotherly love and assistance rather than hate and violence. It is time to observe, objectively and logically, the world situation that has resulted from competition and experiencing the premise of survival of the fittest. This perspective separates humans one from another. Individuals making the choice to pursue a new course of thought will lead the way to different interaction with each other and will in time create a new paradigm of human experience for the planetary whole. It is time to begin.

ORDER ENTIRE SET (Vol. I, II, III) for $19.95.

Sold separately, $6.95 each

The Handbook of the New Paradigm,
Book plus audio CD $6.95

S & H (one book) $2.00; (volume set) $4.00

The Handbook of The New Paradigm Vol. I

ISBN: 1-893157-04-0, 192 pages, mass market paperback

Embracing the Rainbow, Vol. II

ISBN: 1-893157-05-9, 144 pages, mass market paperback

Becoming, Vol. III

ISBN: 1-893157-07-5, 180 pages, mass market paperback

Bonus

Receive "Messages From the Ground Crew" FREE when purchasing the entire set.

Please call 1-800-729-4131 or email: global@nohoax.com

THE SPIRITUAL LAWS AND LESSONS OF THE UNIVERSE

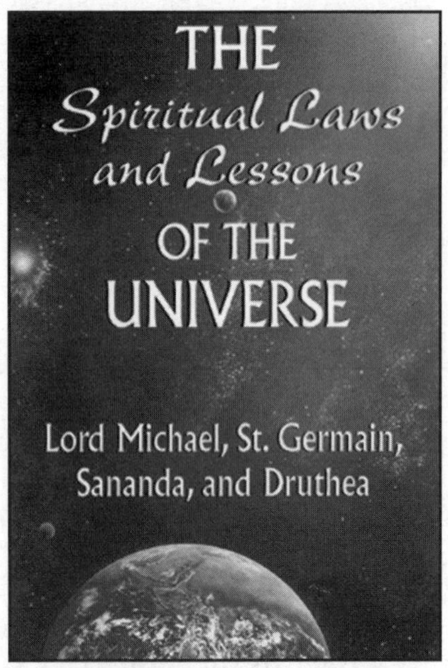

$16.95 ISBN: 0-9640104-6-1 367 pages, trade paper

For eons of time in your human history, mankind has experienced and existed in blindness about his divine spiritual heritage, that is, his oneness with the Creation. Since the time of the "Fall" from "grace," many have continued to struggle with what is "their" purpose, and why it is so difficult to find and know THE TRUTH. Many, in their ignorance and confusion, have asked themselves why the Creator allows the seemingly unending ruthless and merciless inhumanity of man to continue; why HE allows suffering of children, wars, disease and pestilence and corruption. Often ones simply decide there is no Creator, which only keeps ones ever "separate" from KNOWING HIS PRESENCE WITHIN.

"The Spiritual Laws and Lessons" is deliverance of truth to YOU.

The Creator is offering YOU the instructions for reaching the "lighted" path back home to HIM, AND THUS TO ONENESS. You will learn HOW to recognize the Anti-Spirit, (that which is AGAINST the Creator and therefore AGAINST LIFE) within YOU and why through your gift of free-will YOU allowed the Anti-Spirit within your temple. You will learn about what are the "Deadliest" Sins (errors) committed by you and also about the nature of YOUR personal responsibility for ALL consequences and experiences within this manifested physical "illusion."

NOW within these pages bringing forth the EIGHTEEN Logical Cosmic Laws of Balance of The Creation, written in explicit detail with MANY examples given for YOUR careful consideration and recognition of truth. Why? To let there be NO misunderstanding of HOW and WHY you, of humanity, have lost your inner as well as planetary BALANCE. You have broken EVERY law set forth herein and have, therefore, suffered the consequences of your errors against the Creator and against LIFE. You each now have before you YOUR "road map" back home to spiritual wisdom, knowledge and truth. Will YOU see? Will YOU hear? Each ONE of you, being fragments of THE CREATION must and will make this choice: To wisely learn your lessons in truth, abide by the laws and thus EARN your Spiritual UNITY and Freedom within the Kingdom OR continue in the darkness of deception, ignorance and spiritual poverty which will keep you bound in the Anti-Spirit's "illusion" of separation. THIS cycle is about to END. The new cycle will BEGIN anew in the GLORY and Celebration of cleansing within and without of ALL fragments of ANTI-LIFE. WILL YOU JOIN OUR FATHER/MOTHER CREATOR in the Divine Holy Kingdom of LIFE? The Creator awaits your decision. So be it.